EMPLOYMENT PRACTICES SERIES

The Employer's Guide to the Family and Medical Leave Act

www.thefmlaguide.com

EMPLOYMENT PRACTICES SERIES

The Employer's Guide to the Family and Medical Leave Act

Diane M. Pfadenhauer, SPHR, Esq.

DataMotion Publishing, LLC

New York

The Employer's Guide to the Family and Medical Leave Act

Library of Congress Control Number: 2011939015

ISBN: 978-0-9815831-7-4

DataMotion Publishing, LLC
1019 Fort Salonga Road, Suite 10-333
Northport, NY 11768-2209
www.datamotionpublishing.com

Table of Contents

Table of Contents

Table of Contents

About the Author

Diane M. Pfadenhauer, SPHR, Esq.

With over 25 years of experience in human resources and as an attorney, Diane is president of Employment Practices Advisors, Inc. a boutique firm specializing in employment litigation consulting (including workplace investigations and expert witness testimony on human resource practices) and human resource consulting encompassing a broad spectrum of tactical and strategic human resource practices and compliance including interim staff, risk prevention and developing human resource strategies to support business goals and objectives. For the past 10 years she has been a professor in the M.B.A. program at St. Joseph's College in New York. Prior to her position at St. Joseph's, she spent over a decade as an adjunct professor in graduate programs throughout the New York metropolitan area.

An active member in community and professional organizations, Diane is admitted to the New York State Bar. As a member of the National Speaker's Association, she is a frequent speaker and writer and her articles have appeared in industry publications including *HR*

Magazine, HR Advisor, the Journal of Private Equity, Law Technology News, the Journal of Corporate Renewal, and the New York Bar Association. She is certified as a Senior Professional in Human Resources (SPHR) by the Human Resources Certification Institute.

Diane is also the writer of the award winning weblog, ***www.strategichrlawyer.com***, read by over 25,000 unique visitors per month from over 50 countries. She was recently awarded the *New York State Liberty Award* for her Pro Bono work in Louisiana following the devastation of Hurricane Katrina.

Diane received her law degree, *cum laude,* from St. John's University School of Law where she was awarded the ABA/BNA Award for Excellence in the Study of Labor and Employment Law. She is a graduate of New York Institute of Technology's Center for Labor and Industrial Relations where she received her M.S., with *distinction.* She received her B.A. from S.U.N.Y. Potsdam, majoring in Industrial Labor Relations.

About Employment Practices Advisors, Inc.

E mployment Practices Advisors was founded in 2004 by Diane Pfadenhauer after a career of over twenty years in human resources management and employment law. She recognized that as the world of human resources becomes increasingly complex, many organizations lack the resources to employ senior level experts in the field yet have the very same needs of larger employers. In other words, small and mid-sized businesses need a seasoned, well-versed expert, but cannot employ one full time. In addition, larger organizations routinely need outside experts with specific expertise to help them meet their organizational objectives.

All services are performed by human resources professionals whose backgrounds are commensurate with the client's needs. Professionals typically have ten or more years of experience and related bachelor's, master's or law degrees and human resources certification. The professional works closely with the client to understand its particular needs and unique attributes.

Employment Practices Advisors also partners with highly acclaimed law firms and other professional firms in order to promote the seamless coordination of human resources and employment law matters.

Specialities include:

<u>Human Resources Consulting</u> - providing support and/ or specialized projects to organizations in all areas of human resource management.

<u>Strategic Consulting Services</u> - providing services to organizations undergoing strategic transitions (such as mergers, acquisitions, growth, turnaround, bankruptcy) in the areas of compliance and human resources.

<u>Employment Litigation Support</u> - providing support to law firms and in-house counsel in the area of workplace investigations, training, employee complaint/hotline services and expert witness services.

www.epadvisorsinc.com
info@epadvisorsinc.com

Warning–Disclaimer

While this book strives to provide the reader with practical guidance and to provide general education on the topic at hand, it is not a substitute for adequate legal or other professional advice. The opinions within represent the opinions of the authors and editors only and, therefore, should not be construed as a position on the part of any particular organization or entity.

Further, nothing herein should be construed as the rendering of legal or other professional advice and the reader is advised to consult with appropriate counsel for obtaining any advice. By reading this publication, no attorney client relationship exists between the reader and either the author or publisher.

Introduction

The Family and Medical Leave Act of 1993 (FMLA) was enacted on February 5, 1993. It became effective for most employers on August 5, 1993. The United States Department of Labor, Wage and Hour Division issued the final regulations, found at 29 CFR Part 825, in 2009 and the rules became effective on January 16, 2009. These regulations also implement new military family leave entitlements enacted under the National Defense Authorization Act for 2008. The National Defense Authorization Act for 2010 also changes certain provisions of the FMLA.

Recognizing that many families are burdened with family care issues, the FMLA is intended to help employees balance their work and family responsibilities by allowing them to take reasonable unpaid leave for certain family and medical reasons. It also seeks to accommodate the legitimate interests of employers. Over the years, however, many employers have found its rules and regulations to be confusing, burdensome and, at times, overwhelming. All too often, the unsuspecting employer will find itself out of compliance.

Covered employers must provide an eligible employee with up to 12 weeks of unpaid leave each year for any of the following reasons:

- for the birth and care of the newborn child of an employee;
- for placement with the employee of a child for adoption or foster care;
- to care for an immediate family member (spouse, child, or parent) with a serious health condition; or
- to take medical leave when the employee is unable to work because of a serious health condition.

To be eligible for FMLA leave, an employee must have been employed for at least 12 months by the employer and for at least 1,250 hours of service with the employer during the 12 months preceding the leave, and be employed at a worksite at which the employer employs at least 50 employees within 75 miles of the worksite. Employers covered by the FMLA must maintain any preexisting group health coverage for an eligible employee during the FMLA leave period under the same conditions coverage would have been provided if the employee had not taken leave and, once the leave period has concluded, reinstate the employee to the same or an equivalent job with equivalent employment benefits, pay, and other terms and conditions of employment.

If an employee believes that his or her FMLA rights have been violated, the employee may file a complaint with the Department of Labor or file a private lawsuit in federal or state court. If the employer has violated an employee's FMLA rights, the employee is entitled to reimbursement for any monetary loss incurred, equitable relief as appropriate, interest, attorneys' fees, expert witness fees, and court costs. Liquidated damages also may be awarded.

Title I of the FMLA is administered by the U.S. Department of Labor and applies to private sector employers of 50 or more employees, public agencies and certain federal employers and entities, such as the U.S. Postal Service and Postal Regulatory Commission. Title II is administered by the U.S. Office of Personnel Management and applies to civil service employees covered by the annual and sick leave system established under 5 U.S.C. Chapter 63, plus certain employees covered by other federal leave systems.

The FMLA is one of the most difficult of all employment laws to administer. The rules are staggering, the procedures daunting and there are countless areas of confusion and misinterpretation to trick the unwary. Yet many employers try to administer this law on their own.

In order to effectively understand the FMLA, one must understand its myriad of numerous and confusing definitions. While there many lay definitions in everyday conversation, it is important to note that almost every term used in the FMLA is a definitional term. That means that the reader needs to put aside what he or she may think a term means and follow strictly the definitions contained in the statute and the regulations.

1

Coverage

The FMLA permits eligible employees of a covered employer to take job-protected, unpaid leave, or to substitute certain earned or accrued paid time off, for up to a total of 12 workweeks in any 12 months because of the birth of a child and to care for the newborn child, because of the placement of a child with the employee for adoption or foster care, because the employee is needed to care for a family member (child, spouse, or parent) with a serious health condition, because the employee's own serious health condition makes the employee unable to perform the functions of his or her job, or because of any qualifying exigency arising out of the fact that the employee's spouse, son, daughter, or parent is a covered military member on active duty (or has been notified of an impending call or order to active duty) in support of a contingency operation. In addition, eligible employees may take job protected, unpaid leave, or substitute appropriate paid leave if the employee has earned or accrued it, for up to a total of 26 workweeks in a "single 12-month period" to care for a covered servicemember with a serious injury or illness.

In certain instances, FMLA leave may be taken on an intermittent basis rather than all at once, or the employee may work a part-time schedule. An employee on FMLA leave is also entitled to have his/her health benefits continued while on leave as if he/she had continued to work instead of taking the leave. Generally, an employee will be able to continue paying no more than his/her regular employee contribution toward the health benefits plan while on leave. An approved leave under the FMLA is not a qualifying event under COBRA. The employer may recover its share only if the employee does not return to work for a reason other than the serious health condition of the employee or the employee's covered family member, the serious injury or illness of a covered servicemember, or another reason beyond the employee's control.

An employee generally has a right to return to the same or equivalent position with equivalent pay, benefits, and working conditions at the conclusion of the leave. Generally, the taking of FMLA leave cannot result in the loss of any benefit that accrued prior to the start of the leave.

For the most part, an employer has a right to advance notice from the employee. In addition, the employer may require an employee to submit certification to substantiate that the leave is due to the serious health condition of the employee or the employee's covered family member, due to the serious injury or illness of a covered servicemember, or because of a qualifying exigency. Failure to comply with these requirements may result in a delay in the start of FMLA leave. Pursuant to a uniformly applied policy, the employer may also require that an employee present a certification of fitness to return to work when the absence was caused by the employee's own serious health condition. The employer may delay restoring the employee to employment without such certificate relating to the health condition which caused the employee's absence.

Employers

Covered Employer

An employer under the FMLA is one who is engaged in commerce or in any industry or activity affecting commerce that employs 50 or more employees for each working day during each of 20 or more calendar workweeks in the current or preceding calendar year. Employers covered by FMLA also include any person acting, directly or indirectly, in the interest of a covered employer to any of the employees of the employer, any successor in interest of a covered employer, and any public agency. Public agencies are covered employers without regard to the number of employees employed. Public as well as private elementary and secondary schools are also covered employers without regard to the number of employees employed.

For purposes of the FMLA, employers who meet the 50 employee coverage test are deemed to be engaged in commerce or in an industry or activity affecting commerce.

Most of the time, the legal entity that employs the employee is the employer. Thus, a corporation is a single employer rather than its separate establishments or divisions. But, where one corporation has an ownership interest in another corporation, it is a separate employer unless it satisfies the requirements of "joint employment" or "integrated employer" status. When integrated employment status is found, the employees of all of the entities that are integrated will count in determining coverage and employee eligibility. Factors considered in determining whether two or more entities are an integrated employer include, a) common management, b) interrelation between operations, c) centralized control of labor relations, and, d) degree of common ownership/ financial control.

Unfortunately for those in senior management, the definition of "employer" under the FMLA includes persons who act directly or indirectly in the interest of the employer. This definition is similar to the definition of employer under the Fair Labor Standards Act. Thus, individuals such as corporate officers "acting in the interest of an employer" can be individually liable for any violations of the FMLA.

Counting Employees

One is considered an employee under the FMLA in much the same way one would be considered an employee under the Fair Labor Standards Act. While many think of common law or other definitions, the FMLA uses the concept of "to suffer or to permit to work." This is a relatively low threshold and simple knowledge of work done for the employer can be enough for an employee to be considered an employee under the FMLA. In addition, any employee whose name appears on the employer's payroll will be considered employed each working day of the calendar week, and must be counted whether or not any compensation is received for the week. But, it is important to remember that the FMLA only applies to employees who are employed within the United States or its territories.

Employees on paid or unpaid leaves are counted as long as the employer has a reasonable expectation that the employee will return to work. If the employee has been laid off (even if subject to recall), the individual is not counted. Part-time employees, like full-time employees, are considered to be employed each working day of the calendar week, as long as they are maintained on the payroll. But, an employee who does not begin work for an employer until after the first working day of a calendar week, or who terminates employment before the last working day of a calendar week, is not considered employed on each working day of that calendar week.

Private employers are covered if they maintained 50 or more employees on the payroll during 20 or more calendar workweeks (not necessarily consecutive workweeks) in either the current or the preceding calendar year. Once a private employer meets the 50 employees/20 workweeks threshold, the employer remains covered until it reaches a future point where it no longer has employed 50 employees for 20 (nonconsecutive) work-weeks in the current and preceding calendar year. The regulations provide the following example to illustrate this point: if an employer who met the 50 employees/20 workweeks test in the calendar year as of September 1, 2008, subsequently dropped below 50 employees before the end of 2008 and continued to employ fewer than 50 employees in all workweeks throughout calendar year 2009, the employer would continue to be covered throughout calendar year 2009 because it met the coverage criteria for 20 workweeks of the preceding calendar year.

Joint Employers

Two or more businesses that exercise some control over the work or working conditions of the employee may be considered joint employers under the FMLA. These joint employers may even be separate and distinct entities with separate owners, managers, and facilities. Where the employee performs work which simultaneously benefits two or more employers, or works for two or more employers at different times during the workweek, a joint employment relationship generally will be considered to exist in situations where, a) the employers have an arrangement to share an employee's services or to interchange employees, b) one employer acts directly or indirectly in the interest of the other employer in relation to the employee, or, c) the employers are not completely disassociated with respect to the employee's employment and may be deemed to share control of the employee, directly or indirectly, because one employer controls, is controlled by, or is under common control with the other employer.

Joint employment will ordinarily be found when a temporary placement agency supplies employees to a second employer. Whether a Professional Employer Organizations (PEO) can be found to have joint employer status with a client employer depends upon the facts and circumstances of the relationship with the client employer. When a PEO performs merely administrative functions, joint status will not be typically found. But, if the PEO has the right to hire, fire, assign, or direct and control the client's employees, or benefits from the work that the employees perform, such rights may lead to a determination that the PEO would be a joint employer with the client employer, depending upon all the facts and circumstances.

When joint employment status is found, the primary employer is the one that is obligated to give required notices and maintain health insurance under the FMLA. The primary employer is determined by looking to the employer that has the authority/responsibility to hire and fire, assign/place the employee, make payroll, and provide employment benefits. For employees of temporary placement agencies, for example, the placement agency most commonly would be the primary employer. Where a PEO is a joint employer, the client employer most commonly would be the primary employer.

Employees jointly employed by two employers must be counted by both employers, whether or not maintained on one of the employer's payroll, in determining employer coverage and employee eligibility. The regulations provide the following example to illustrate this point: an employer who jointly employs 15 workers from a temporary placement agency and 40 permanent workers is covered by FMLA. An employee on leave who is working for a secondary employer is considered employed by the secondary employer, and must be counted for coverage and eligibility purposes, as long as the employer has a reasonable expectation that the employee will return to employment with that employer. In those cases in which a PEO is determined to be a joint employer of a client employer's employees, the client employer would only be required to count employees of the PEO (or employees of other clients of the PEO) if the client employer jointly employed those employees.

The primary employer is responsible for job restoration. The secondary employer is responsible for accepting the employee returning from FMLA leave in place of the replacement employee if the secondary employer continues to utilize an employee from the temporary placement agency, and the agency chooses to place the employee with the secondary employer. A secondary employer is also responsible for compliance with the prohibited acts provisions with respect to its jointly employed employees, whether or not the secondary employer is covered by FMLA. The prohibited acts include prohibitions against interfering with an employee's attempt to exercise rights under the Act, or discharging or discriminating against an employee for opposing a practice which is unlawful under FMLA. A covered secondary employer will be responsible for compliance with all the provisions of the FMLA with respect to its regular, permanent workforce.

Successors in Interest

The FMLA looks generally to definitions under Title VII of the Civil Rights Act and the Vietnam Era Veterans' Readjustment and Assistance Act for guidance in determining whether an employer is covered because it is a "successor in interest" to a covered employer. But, unlike Title VII, whether the successor has notice of the employee's claim is not a consideration. Notice may be relevant, however, in determining successor liability for violations of the predecessor. Factors to be considered to determine whether an employer will be considered a successor in interest include, a) substantial continuity of the same business operations, b) use of the same plant, c) continuity of the work force, d) similarity of jobs and working conditions, e) similarity of supervisory personnel, f) similarity in machinery, g) equipment, and production methods, h) similarity of products or services, and, i) the ability of the predecessor to provide relief.

When an employer is found to be a successor in interest, the employees' entitlements arc the same as if the employment by the predecessor and successor were continuous employment by a single employer. A successor employer that meets the FMLA's coverage criteria must count periods of employment and hours worked for the predecessor for purposes of determining employee eligibility for FMLA leave.

Determining Whether 50 Employees are Employed Within 75 Miles

A worksite can refer to either a single location or a group of contiguous locations. This may include, for example, a campus or industrial park, or separate facilities in proximity with one another. There may be several single sites of employment within a single building if separate employers conduct activities within the building. For example, an office building with 50 different businesses as tenants will contain 50 sites of employment. The offices of each employer will be considered separate sites of employment for purposes of FMLA.

An employee's worksite will ordinarily be the site the employee reports to or from which the work is assigned. Separate buildings or areas which are not directly connected or in immediate proximity can also be considered a single worksite particularly if they are in reasonable geographic proximity, are used for the same purpose, and share the same staff and equipment. Thus, if an employer manages a number of warehouses in a metropolitan area but regularly shifts or rotates the same employees from one building to another, the multiple warehouses would be considered a single worksite. For employees with no fixed worksite (such as, for example, construction workers, drivers, and salespersons), their worksite is the site which is considered their home base, from where their work is assigned or to site to which they report.

When joint employment status is found, an employee's worksite is the primary employer's office from which the employee is assigned or reports, unless the employee has physically worked for at least one year at a facility of a secondary employer, in which case the employee's worksite is that location. The employee is also counted by the secondary employer to determine eligibility for the secondary employer's full-time or permanent employees.

The 75-mile distance is measured by surface miles, using surface transportation over public streets, roads, highways and waterways, by the shortest route from the facility where the employee needing leave is employed. Absent available surface transportation between worksites, the distance is measured by using the most frequently utilized mode of transportation.

The determination of how many employees are employed within 75 miles of the worksite is based on the number of employees maintained on the payroll.

Employees

Eligible Employees

An eligible employee is an employee who, a) has been employed by the employer for at least 12 months (which generally need not have been consecutive, but subject to certain limited exceptions), and has been employed for at least 1,250 hours of service during the 12-month period immediately preceding the commencement of the leave, and, b) is employed at a worksite where 50 or more employees are employed by the employer within 75 miles of that worksite.

In order to determine if an employee has worked the required 1,250 hours, the FMLA once again looks to the Fair Labor Standards Act. Specifically, the determining factor is the number of hours an employee has worked for the employer within the meaning of the FLSA.

In accordance with the Uniformed Services Employment and Reemployment Rights Act (USERRA), an employee returning from military obligations must be credited with the hours of work that would have been performed but for the period of military service. One who is returning from the military has the benefit of having the hours that would have been worked for the employer, but for the military service, added to his/her hours actually worked during the previous 12-month period in calculating the 1,250 hour requirement. Determining what hours the individual would have worked is done by looking at his/her pre-service work schedule.

In some instances an employer may not have accurate records of hours worked. This may be a result of correctly classifying employees as exempt under the Fair Labor Standards Act or perhaps due to poor record keeping. In either circumstance, the employer is the one who bears the burden of demonstrating that the employee did not work the requisite 1,250 hours.

The calculation of the 1,250 hours and the 12 months is made as of the date the FMLA leave starts. Thus, for example, if an employee is on a "non-FMLA leave" at the time he or she meets the eligibility requirements, any portion of the leave taken for an FMLA qualifying reason after the employee meets the eligibility requirement would be FMLA leave. But, whether 50 employees are employed within 75 miles to determine an employee's eligibility for FMLA benefits is determined when the employee gives notice of the need for leave (not when it starts). Once an employee is determined eligible in response to his/her notice of the need for leave, the employee's eligibility is not affected by any subsequent change in the number of employees employed at or within 75 miles of the employee's worksite.

In addition, an employer is prohibited from terminating an already approved leave, which may or may not have already begun, if the employer's employee count falls below 50. The regulations provide the following example to illustrate this point: if an employer employs 60 employees in August, but expects that the number of employees will drop to 40 in December, the employer must grant FMLA benefits to an otherwise eligible employee who gives notice of the need for leave in August for a period of leave to begin in December.

It should go without saying that the right to take FMLA leave applies equally to male and female employees.

In a situation where the employee's employment status has been interrupted (i.e. in the event of a layoff), the employee must return to active status in order to be eligible for FMLA leave.

Types of Leave

Own or Family Member's Serious Health Condition

Generally, a "serious health condition" entitling an employee to FMLA leave means an illness, injury, impairment or physical or mental condition that involves inpatient care or continuing treatment by a health care provider. These terms are more fully described below. The term "incapacity" means inability to work, attend school or perform other regular daily activities due to the serious health condition, treatment of the serious health condition of recovery therefrom. The term "treatment" includes (but is not limited to) examinations to determine if a serious health condition exists and evaluations of the condition. Treatment does not include routine physical examinations, eye examinations, or dental examinations. A regimen of continuing treatment includes, for example, a course of prescription medication (such as antibiotics) or therapy requiring special equipment to resolve or alleviate the health condition (such as oxygen). A regimen of continuing treatment that includes the taking of over-the-counter medications (such as aspirin, antihistamines, or salves); or bed rest, drinking fluids, exercise, and other similar activities that can be initiated without a visit to a health care provider, is not, by itself, sufficient to constitute a regimen of continuing treatment for the purposes of FMLA leave.

Conditions for which cosmetic treatments are administered (such as most treatments for acne or plastic surgery) are not serious health conditions unless inpatient hospital care is required or unless complications develop. Ordinarily, unless complications arise, conditions such as the common cold, the flu, ear aches, upset stomach, minor ulcers, headaches other than migraines, routine dental or orthodontia problems, periodontal disease, and the like, are examples of conditions that do not meet the definition of a serious health condition and do not qualify for FMLA leave. Restorative dental or plastic surgery after an injury or removal of cancerous growths can be considered a serious health condition. Mental illness or allergies may also be considered serious health conditions.

Inpatient care means an overnight stay in a hospital, hospice, or residential medical care facility, including any period of incapacity or any subsequent treatment in connection with that inpatient care.

A serious health condition involving continuing treatment by a health care provider includes any one or more of the following:

1. Incapacity and Treatment. A period of incapacity of more than three consecutive, full calendar days, and any subsequent treatment or period of incapacity relating to the same condition, that also involves, a) treatment two or more times, within 30 days of the first day of incapacity (unless extenuating circumstances exist) by a health care provider, by a nurse under direct supervision of a health care provider, or by a provider of health care services (such as a physical therapist) under orders of, or on referral by, a health care provider, or, b) treatment by a health care provider on at least one occasion, which results in a regimen of continuing treatment under the su-

pervision of the health care provider. Treatment by a health care provider means an in-person visit to a health care provider. The first (or only) in-person treatment visit must take place within seven days of the first day of incapacity. Whether additional treatment visits or a regimen of continuing treatment is necessary within the 30-day period is determined by the health care provider. Extenuating circumstances means circumstances beyond the employee's control that prevent the follow-up visit from occurring as planned by the health care provider. Whether a given set of circumstances are extenuating depends on the facts. For example, extenuating circumstances exist if a health care provider determines that a second in-person visit is needed within the 30-day period, but the health care provider does not have any available appointments during that time period.

2. <u>Pregnancy or Prenatal Care</u>. Any period of incapacity due to pregnancy, or for prenatal care.

3. <u>Chronic Conditions</u>. Chronic conditions include any period of incapacity or treatment for such incapacity due to a chronic serious health condition. A chronic serious health condition is one which, a) requires periodic visits (defined as at least twice a year) for treatment by a health care provider, or by a nurse under direct supervision of a health care provider, b) continues over an extended period of time (including recurring episodes of a single underlying condition); and, c) may cause episodic rather than a continuing period of incapacity (such as, for example, asthma, diabetes, or epilepsy).

4. <u>Permanent or Long-Term Conditions</u>. These concern a period of incapacity which is permanent or long-term due to a condition for which treatment may not be effective. The employee or family member must be under the continuing supervision of, but need not be receiving active treatment by, a health care provider. Examples include Alzheimer's disease, a severe stroke, or the terminal stages of a disease.

5. <u>Conditions Requiring Multiple Treatments</u>. These refer to any period of absence to receive multiple treatments (including any related period of recovery) by a health care provider or by a provider of health care services under orders of, or on referral by, a health care provider, for: a) restorative surgery after an accident or other injury; or 2) a condition that would likely result in a period of incapacity of more than three consecutive, full calendar days in the absence of medical intervention or treatment, such as cancer (such as chemotherapy or radiation), severe arthritis (physical therapy), or kidney disease (dialysis).

Absences attributable to incapacity qualify for FMLA leave even though the employee or the covered family member does not receive treatment from a health care provider during the absence, and even if the absence does not last more than three consecutive, full calendar days. For example, an employee with asthma may be unable to report for work due to the onset of an asthma attack or because the employee's health care provider has advised the employee to stay home when the pollen count exceeds a certain level. An employee who is pregnant may be unable to report to work because of severe morning sickness.

Treatment of Substance Abuse

To the extent that substance abuse meets the definitions of incapacity, treatment, inpatient care, or continuing treatment defined elsewhere in this guide, it may also be considered a serious health condition thereby enabling an individual to take FMLA leave. However, FMLA leave may only be taken for treatment for substance abuse by a health care provider or by a provider of health care services on referral by a health care provider. Absence because of the employee's use (or abuse) of the substance, rather than for treatment, does not qualify for FMLA leave.

Notwithstanding the foregoing, treatment for substance abuse does not prevent an employer from taking employment action against an employee pursuant to an established policy, applied in a nondiscriminatory manner that has been communicated to all employees, that provides under certain circumstances an employee may be terminated for substance abuse. This is true whether or not the employee is presently taking FMLA leave. The employer may not, however, take action against the employee because the employee has exercised his or her right to take FMLA leave for treatment. An employee may also take FMLA leave to care for a covered family member who is receiving treatment for substance abuse. The employer may not take action against an employee who is providing care for a covered family member receiving treatment for substance abuse.

Pregnancy or Birth

Both the mother and father are entitled to FMLA leave for the birth of their child. Both the mother and father are entitled to FMLA leave to bond with the healthy newborn child during the 12-month period beginning on the date of birth. An employee's entitlement to FMLA leave for a birth expires at the end of the 12-month period beginning on the date of the birth. If State law allows, or the employer permits, bonding leave to be taken beyond this period, such leave will not qualify as FMLA leave.

When a husband and wife are covered by the same employer, a different rule applies. The husband and wife may be limited to a combined total of 12 weeks of leave during any 12-month period if the leave is taken for birth of the employee's child or to care for the child after birth, for placement of a child with the employee for adoption or foster care or to care for the child after placement, or to care for the employee's parent with a serious health condition. This limitation on the total weeks of leave applies to leave taken for the reasons specified as long as a husband and wife are employed by the same employer. It would apply, for example, even though the spouses are employed at two different worksites of an employer located more than 75 miles from each other, or by two different operating divisions of the same company. On the other hand, if one spouse is ineligible for FMLA leave, the other spouse would be entitled to a full 12 weeks of FMLA leave. Where the husband and wife both use a portion of the total 12-week FMLA leave entitlement for either the birth of a child, for placement for adoption or foster care, or to care for a parent, the husband and wife would each be entitled to the difference between the amount he or she has taken individually and 12 weeks for FMLA leave for other purposes. The regulations provide the following example to illustrate this point: if each spouse took 6 weeks of leave to care for a healthy, newborn child, each could use an additional 6 weeks due to his or her own serious health condition or to care for a child with a serious health condition.

Many State pregnancy disability laws specify a period of disability either before or after the birth of a child. These periods of disability would also be considered FMLA leave for a serious health condition of the mother and would not be subject to the combined limit.

The mother typically experiences her own serious health condition and is, therefore, entitled to FMLA leave for incapacity due to pregnancy, for prenatal care, or for her own serious health condition following the birth of the child. Circumstances may require that FMLA leave begin before the actual date of birth of a child. An expectant mother may take FMLA leave before the birth of the child for prenatal care or if her condition makes her unable to work. She is entitled to leave for incapacity due to pregnancy even though she does not receive treatment from a health care provider during the absence, and even if the absence does not last for more than three consecutive calendar days. For example, a pregnant employee may be unable to report to work because of severe morning sickness.

A husband may be entitled to FMLA leave if needed to care for his pregnant spouse who is incapacitated or if needed to care for her during her prenatal care or if needed to care for the spouse following the birth of a child if the spouse has a serious health condition.

In the event a child, including a newborn, has a serious health condition, both the mother and father are entitled to FMLA leave. The husband and the wife may each take 12 weeks of FMLA leave if needed to care for their newborn child with a serious health condition, even if both are employed by the same employer, provided they have not exhausted their entitlements during the applicable 12-month FMLA leave period.

With respect to intermittent and reduced schedule leave, an employer may refuse to agree to permit an employee to take such leave to be with a healthy newborn child. The regulations provide the following example as an illustration of this point: an employer and employee may agree to a part-time work schedule after the birth. If the employer agrees to permit intermittent or reduced schedule leave for the birth of a child, the employer may require the employee to transfer temporarily, during the period the intermittent or reduced schedule leave is required, to an available alternative position for which the employee is qualified and which better accommodates recurring periods of leave than does the employee's regular position. Transfer to an alternative position may require compliance with any applicable collective bargaining agreement, federal law (such as the Americans with Disabilities Act), and State law. Transfer to an alternative position may include altering an existing job to better accommodate the employee's need for intermittent or reduced leave. The employer's agreement is not required for intermittent leave required by the serious health condition of the mother or newborn child.

Adoption or Foster Care

Employees are entitled to FMLA leave for placement with the employee of a child for adoption or foster care. They are permitted to take FMLA leave before the actual placement or adoption of a child if an absence from work is required for the placement for adoption or foster care to proceed. For example, the employee may be required to attend counseling sessions, appear in court, consult with his or her attorney or the doctor(s) representing the birth parent, submit to a physical examination, or travel to another country or state to complete an adoption. The source of an adopted child is not a factor in determining eligibility for leave.

Similar to leave for the birth of a child, an employee's entitlement to leave for adoption or foster care expires at the end of the 12-month period beginning on the date of the placement. If State law allows, or the employer permits and leave for adoption or foster care is to be taken beyond this period, that leave will not qualify as FMLA leave. The employee is entitled to FMLA leave even if the adopted or foster child does not have a serious health condition.

With regard to a situation where a husband and wife who are both eligible for FMLA leave and are employed by the same covered employer, the two may be limited to a combined total of 12 weeks of leave during any 12-month period if the leave is taken for the placement of the employee's child or to care for the child after placement, for the birth of the employee's child or to care for the child after birth, or to care for the employee's parent with a serious health condition. This limitation on the total weeks of leave applies to leave taken for the reasons specified as long as a husband and wife are employed by the "same employer." It would apply, for example, even though the spouses are employed at two different worksites of an employer located more than 75 miles from each other, or by two different operating divisions of the same company. On the other hand, if one spouse is ineligible for FMLA leave, the other spouse would be entitled to a full 12 weeks of FMLA leave. Where the husband and wife both use a portion of the total 12-week FMLA leave entitlement for either the birth of a child, for placement for adoption or foster care, or to care for a parent, the husband and wife would each be entitled to the difference between the amount he or she has taken individually and 12 weeks for FMLA leave for other purposes. For example, if each spouse took 6 weeks of leave to care for a healthy, newly placed child, each could use an additional 6 weeks due to his or her own serious health condition or to care for a child with a serious health condition.

An eligible employee is generally entitled to FMLA leave in order to care for an adopted or foster child with a serious health condition. Thus, a husband and wife may each take 12 weeks of FMLA leave if needed to care for an adopted or foster child with a serious health condition, even if both are employed by the same employer, provided they have not exhausted their entitlements during the applicable 12-month FMLA leave period.

An eligible employee may use intermittent or reduced schedule leave after the placement of a healthy child for adoption or foster care only if the employer agrees. Thus, for example, the employer and employee may agree to a part-time work schedule after the placement for bonding purposes. If the employer agrees to permit intermittent or reduced schedule leave for the placement for adoption or foster care, the employer may require the employee to transfer temporarily, during the period the intermittent or reduced schedule leave is required, to an available alternative position for which the employee is qualified and which better accommodates recurring periods of leave than does the employee's regular position. Transfer to an alternative position may require compliance with any applicable collective bargaining agreement, federal law (such as the Americans with Disabilities Act), and State law. Transfer to an alternative position may include altering an existing job to better accommodate the employee's need for intermittent or reduced leave. The employer's agreement is not required for intermittent leave required by the serious health condition of the adopted or foster child.

Care for a Parent

Generally, an eligible employee is entitled to FMLA leave if needed to care for the employee's parent (not a parent-in-law) with a serious health condition. This leave, like other leaves, is subject to the same employer limitations previously described. Thus, if a husband and wife who are eligible for FMLA leave and are employed by the same covered employer may be limited to a combined total of 12 weeks of leave during any 12-month period if the leave is taken to care for the employee's parent with a serious health condition, for the birth of

44

the employee's son or daughter or to care for the child after the birth, or for placement of a son or daughter with the employee for adoption or foster care or to care for the child after placement. This limitation on the total weeks of leave applies to leave taken for the reasons specified as long as a husband and wife are employed by the "same employer." It would apply, for example, even though the spouses are employed at two different worksites of an employer located more than 75 miles from each other, or by two different operating divisions of the same company. On the other hand, if one spouse is ineligible for FMLA leave, the other spouse would be entitled to a full 12 weeks of FMLA leave. Where the husband and wife both use a portion of the total 12-week FMLA leave entitlement for either the birth of a child, for placement for adoption or foster care, or to care for a parent, the husband and wife would each be entitled to the difference between the amount he or she has taken individually and 12 weeks for FMLA leave for other purposes. For example, if each spouse took 6 weeks of leave to care for a parent, each could use an additional 6 weeks due to his or her own serious health condition or to care for a child with a serious health condition.

Qualifying Exigency

Prior to the passage of the National Defense Authorization Act for 2010 (NDAA), an eligible employee could take qualifying exigency leave only when his or her son, daughter or parent was a member of the Reserves or National Guard and had been called up to active duty or notified of an impending call or order to active duty in support of a "contingency operation." Qualifying exigency leave was not permitted for employees with family members who were active members of the Armed Forces.

As a result of the passage of the NDAA, qualifying exigency leave has been expanded to permit an eligible employee to take FMLA leave for a qualifying exigency related to the deployment of a son, daughter or parent who is a member of a regular component of the Armed Forces. In addition, the call to active duty or notice of an impending call or order to active duty is no longer limited to those related to "contingency operations." Instead, covered active duty now relates to when a member of the regular or reserve components of the Armed Forces is deployed to any foreign country. Such eligible employees may take FMLA leave for one or more of the following qualifying exigencies:

Short-Notice Deployment

This leave may be taken for the purpose of addressing any issue that arises from the fact that a covered military member is notified of an impending call or order to active duty in support of a contingency operation seven or less calendar days prior to the date of deployment. FMLA leave for short-notice deployment can be used for a period of seven calendar days beginning on the date a covered military member is notified of an impending call or order to active duty in support of a contingency operation.

Military Events and Related Activities

This type of leave may be taken, a) to attend any official ceremony, program, or event sponsored by the military that is related to the active duty or call to active duty status of a covered military member, and b) to attend family support or assistance programs and informational briefings sponsored or promoted by the military, military service organizations, or the American Red Cross that are related to the active duty or call to active duty status of a covered military member.

Childcare and School Activities

Such leave may be taken:

1. to arrange for alternative childcare when the active duty or call to active duty status of a covered military member necessitates a change in the existing childcare arrangement for a biological, adopted, or foster child, a stepchild, or a legal ward of a covered military member, or a child for whom a covered military member stands in loco parentis, who is either under age 18, or age 18 or older and incapable of self-care because of a mental or physical disability at the time that FMLA leave is to commence,

2. to provide childcare on an urgent, immediate need basis (but not on a routine, regular, or everyday basis) when the need to provide such care arises from the active duty or call to active duty status of a covered military member for a biological, adopted, or foster child, a stepchild, or a legal ward of a covered military member, or a child for whom a covered military member stands in loco parentis, who is either under age 18, or age 18 or older and incapable of self-care because of a mental or physical disability

at the time that FMLA leave is to commence,

3. to enroll in or transfer to a new school or day care facility a biological, adopted, or foster child, a stepchild, or a legal ward of the covered military member, or a child for whom the covered military member stands in loco parentis, who is either under age 18, or age 18 or older and incapable of self-care because of a mental or physical disability at the time that FMLA leave is to commence, when enrollment or transfer is necessitated by the active duty or call to active duty status of a covered military member, or,

4. to attend meetings with staff at a school or a day care facility, such as meetings with school officials regarding disciplinary measures, parent-teacher conferences, or meetings with school counselors, for a biological, adopted, or foster child, a stepchild, or a legal ward of the covered military member, or a child for whom the covered military member stands in loco parentis, who is either under age 18, or age 18 or older and incapable of self-care because of a mental or physical disability at the time that FMLA leave is to commence, when such meetings are necessary due to circumstances arising from the active duty or call to active duty status of a covered military member.

Financial and Legal Arrangements

The purpose of this leave is to address the covered military member's absence while on active duty or call to active duty status, such as preparing and executing financial and health care powers of attorney, transferring bank account signature authority, enrolling in the Defense Enrollment Eligibility Reporting System (DEERS), obtaining military identification cards, or preparing or updating a will or living trust. In addition, leave may be taken to act as the covered military member's representative before a federal, state, or local agency for purposes of obtaining, arranging, or appealing military service benefits while the covered military member is on active duty or call to active duty status, and for a period of 90 days following the termination of the covered military member's active duty status.

Counseling

This leave be taken to attend counseling provided by someone other than a health care provider for oneself, for the covered military member, or for the biological, adopted, or foster child, a stepchild, or a legal ward of the covered military member, or a child for whom the covered military member stands in loco parentis, who is either under age 18, or age 18 or older and incapable of self-care because of a mental or physical disability at the time that FMLA leave is to commence, provided that the need for counseling arises from the active duty or call to active duty status of a covered military member,

Rest and Recuperation

Leave for this purpose may be taken in order to spend time with a covered military member who is on short-term, temporary, rest and recuperation leave during the period of deployment. In this instance, eligible employees may take up to five days of leave for each instance of rest and recuperation.

Post-Deployment Activities

This type of leave may be taken in order to attend arrival ceremonies, reintegration briefings and events, and any other official ceremony or program sponsored by the military for a period of 90 days following the termination of the covered military member's active duty status. This may also include addressing issues that arise from the death of a covered military member while on active duty status, such as meeting and recovering the body of the covered military member and making funeral arrangements.

The employer and employee agree that any additional activities will qualify as an exigency, and agree to both the timing and duration of such leave.

A "covered military member" means the employee's spouse, son, daughter, or parent on active duty or call to active duty status. A "son or daughter on active duty or call to active duty status" means the employee's biological, adopted, or foster child, stepchild, legal ward, or a child for whom the employee stood in loco parentis, who is on active duty or call to active duty status, and who is of any age.

"Active duty or call to active duty status" means duty under a call or order to active duty (or notification of an impending call or order to active duty) in support of a contingency operation pursuant to various sections of the United States Code which authorize the order to active duty of retired members of the Armed Forces, retired members of the Reserve, all Reservists, any other member of the Ready Reserve, Selected Reserve, Individual Ready Reserve or National Guard.

Employees are eligible to take FMLA leave because of a qualifying exigency when the covered military member is on active duty or call to active duty status in support of a contingency operation as either a member of the reserve components (Army National Guard of the United States, Army Reserve, Navy Reserve, Marine Corps Reserve, Air National Guard of the United States, Air Force Reserve and Coast Guard Reserve), or a retired member of the Regular Armed Forces or Reserve. An employee whose family member is on active duty or call to active duty status in support of a contingency operation as a member of the Regular Armed Forces is eligible to take leave because of a qualifying exigency.

A call to active duty for purposes of leave taken because of a qualifying exigency refers to a Federal call to active duty. State calls to active duty are not covered unless under order of the President of the United States in support of a contingency operation.

The active duty orders of a covered military member will generally specify if the servicemember is serving in support of a contingency operation by citation to the relevant section of the United States Code and/or by reference to the specific name of the contingency operation. A military operation qualifies as a contingency operation if it: a) is designated by the Secretary of Defense as an operation in which members of the armed forces are or may become involved in military actions, operations, or hostilities against an enemy of the United States or against an opposing military force; or b) results in the call or order to, or retention on, active duty of members of the uniformed services under relevant sections of Title 10 of the United States Code or any other provision of law during a war or during a national emergency declared by the President or Congress.

Military Caregiver Leave or Care for a Covered Servicemember with a Serious Injury or Illness

Eligible employees are entitled to FMLA leave to care for a current member of the Armed Forces, including a member of the National Guard or Reserves, or a member of the Armed Forces, the National Guard or Reserves who is on the temporary disability retired list, who has a serious injury or illness incurred in the line of duty on active duty for which he or she is recuperation, or therapy; or otherwise in outpatient status; or otherwise on the temporary disability retired list. Under the National Defense Authorization Act for 2010 (NDAA), the definition of a "covered servicemember" has been expanded to include a veteran who is undergoing medical treatment, recuperation or therapy for a serious injury or illness and who was a member of the Armed Forces, including the National Guard and Reserves, at any time during the five-year period preceding the date on which the veteran undergoes medical treatment, recuperation or therapy.

Serious injury or illness means an injury or illness incurred by a covered servicemember in the line of duty

on active duty that may render the servicemember medically unfit to perform the duties of his or her office,
grade, rank or rating. This definition was also expanded by the NDAA for 2010 to include an injury or illness
that was incurred by the covered servicemember prior
to her or his active duty and was aggravated by service
in the line of duty while on active duty. A serious injury
or illness of a veteran is further defined to encompass
an injury or illness incurred in the line of duty while
on active duty, or which existed prior to active duty but
was aggravated by service in line of duty while on active duty, and that manifested itself either before or
after the covered servicemember became a veteran.

Outpatient status, with respect to a covered servicemember, means the status of a member of the Armed
Forces assigned to either a military medical treatment
facility as an outpatient; or a unit established for the
purpose of providing command and control of members
of the Armed Forces receiving medical care as outpatients.

In order to care for a covered servicemember, an eligible employee must be the spouse, son or daughter
(the covered servicemember's biological, adopted, or
foster child, stepchild, legal ward, or a child for whom
the covered servicemember stood in loco parentis, and
who is of any age), parent (the covered servicemember's
biological, adoptive, step or foster father or mother,
or any other individual who stood in loco parentis to
the covered servicemember, not including parents "in
law"), or next of kin of a covered servicemember. The
"next of kin of a covered servicemember" is the nearest
blood relative, other than the covered servicemember's

spouse, parent, son, or daughter, in the following order of priority: blood relatives who have been granted legal custody of the servicemember by court decree or statutory provisions, brothers and sisters, grandparents, aunts and uncles, and first cousins, unless the covered servicemember has specifically designated in writing another blood relative as his or her nearest blood relative for purposes of military caregiver leave under the FMLA.

With regard to next of kin, when no such designation is made, and there are multiple family members with the same level of relationship to the covered servicemember, all of these family members may be considered the covered servicemember's next of kin and may take FMLA leave to provide care to the covered servicemember, either consecutively or simultaneously. When such designation has been made, the designated individual shall be deemed to be the covered servicemember's only next of kin. The regulations provide the following example to illustrate this point: if a covered servicemember has three siblings and has not designated a blood relative to provide care, all three siblings would be considered the covered servicemember's next of kin. Alternatively, where a covered servicemember has a sibling(s) and designates a cousin as his or her next of kin for FMLA purposes, then only the designated cousin is eligible as the covered servicemember's next of kin. An employer is permitted to require an employee to provide confirmation of covered family relationship to the covered servicemember.

Unlike the traditional 12 weeks of unpaid leave under the FMLA, for these purposes an eligible employee is entitled to 26 workweeks of leave to care for a covered servicemember with a serious injury or illness during a single 12-month period, which begins on the first day the eligible employee takes FMLA leave to care for a covered servicemember and ends 12 months after that date, regardless of the method used by the employer to determine the employee's 12 workweeks of leave entitlement for other FMLA-qualifying reasons. If an eligible employee does not take all of his or her 26 workweeks of leave entitlement to care for a covered servicemember during this single 12-month period, the remaining part of his or her 26 workweeks of leave entitlement to care for the covered servicemember is forfeited. This 26-week leave is applied on a per-covered servicemember, per-injury basis. This means that an eligible employee may be entitled to take more than one period of 26 workweeks of leave if the leave is to care for different covered servicemembers or to care for the same servicemember with a subsequent serious injury or illness, except that no more than 26 workweeks of leave may be taken within any single 12-month period. An eligible employee may take more than one period of 26 workweeks of leave to care for a covered servicemember with more than one serious injury or illness only when the serious injury or illness is a subsequent serious injury or illness. When an eligible employee takes leave to care for more than one covered servicemember or for a subsequent serious injury or illness of the same covered servicemember, and the single 12-month periods corresponding to the different military caregiver leave entitlements overlap, the employee is limited to taking no more than 26 workweeks of leave in each single 12-month period.

When combining the leave to care for a covered service-member with other types of FMLA leave, an eligible employee is entitled to a combined total of 26 workweeks of leave for any FMLA-qualifying reason during the single 12-month period, provided that the employee is entitled to no more than 12 weeks of leave for one or more of the following: because of the birth of a son or daughter of the employee and in order to care for such son or daughter; because of the placement of a son or daughter with the employee for adoption or foster care; in order to care for the spouse, son, daughter, or parent with a serious health condition; because of the employee's own serious health condition; or because of a qualifying exigency. This means, for example, an employee may, during the single 12-month period, take 16 weeks of FMLA leave to care for a covered servicemember and 10 weeks of FMLA leave to care for a newborn child. However, the employee may not take more than 12 weeks of FMLA leave to care for the newborn child during the single 12-month period, even if the employee takes fewer than 14 weeks of FMLA leave to care for a covered service-member.

Regardless whether the leave is for a covered service-member or for any other reason permitted under the FMLA, the employer is responsible for designating leave, paid or unpaid, as FMLA-qualifying, and for giving notice of the designation to the employee. In the case of leave that qualifies as both leave to care for a covered servicemember and leave to care for a family member with a serious health condition during the single 12-month period, the employer must designate such leave as leave to care for a covered servicemem-ber first. Leave that qualifies as both leave to care for a covered servicemember and leave taken to care for a family member with a serious health condition during the single 12-month period must not be designated and counted as both leave to care for a covered servicemember and leave to care for a family member with a serious health condition. As is the case with leave taken for other qualifying reasons, employers may retroactively designate leave as leave to care for a covered servicemember.

When a husband and wife are both eligible for FMLA leave and are employed by the same employer, they may be limited to a combined total of 26 workweeks of leave during the single 12-month period if the leave is taken for birth of the employee's son or daughter or to care for the child after birth, for placement of a son or daughter with the employee for adoption or foster care, or to care for the child after placement, to care for the employee's parent with a serious health condition, or to care for a covered servicemember with a serious injury or illness. This limitation on the total weeks of leave applies to leave taken for the reasons specified as long as a husband and wife are employed by the same employer. It would apply, for example, even though the spouses are employed at two different worksites of an employer located more than 75 miles from each other, or by two different operating divisions of the same company. On the other hand, if one spouse is ineligible for FMLA leave, the other spouse would be entitled to a full 26 workweeks of FMLA leave.

Definitional Terms Related to Types of Leave

Serious Health Condition

A "serious health condition" which entitles an employee to FMLA leave is defined as an illness, injury, impairment or physical or mental condition that involves in-patient care or continuing treatment by a health care provider.

Incapacity means the inability to work, attend school or perform other regular daily activities due to the serious health condition, or treatment for or the recovery from the serious health condition.

Treatment includes (but is not limited to) examinations to determine if a serious health condition exists and evaluations of the condition. Treatment does not, however, include routine physical examinations, eye examinations, or dental examinations. A regimen of continuing treatment includes, for example, a course of prescription medication (including, for example, antibiotics) or therapy requiring special equipment to resolve or alleviate the health condition (such as oxygen). A regimen of continuing treatment that includes the taking of over-the-counter medications (such as aspirin, antihistamines, or salves); or bed rest, drinking fluids, exercise, and other similar activities that can be initiated without a visit to a health care provider, is not, by itself, sufficient to constitute a regimen of continuing treatment for purposes of FMLA leave.

Cosmetic conditions, for which cosmetic treatments are provided, such as acne treatments or plastic surgery, are not serious health conditions unless inpatient hospital care is required or unless complications develop. Ordinarily, unless complications arise, the common cold, the flu, ear aches, upset stomach, minor ulcers, headaches other than migraine, routine dental or orthodontia problems, periodontal disease, etc., are examples of conditions that do not meet the definition of a serious health condition and do not qualify for FMLA leave. Restorative dental or plastic surgery after an injury or removal of cancerous growths can be considered serious health conditions provided all the other conditions of this regulation are met. Mental illness or allergies may also be considered serious health under certain circumstances.

Inpatient Care

Inpatient care means an overnight stay in a hospital, hospice, or residential medical care facility or any subsequent treatment in connection with that inpatient care.

Continuing Treatment

A serious health condition involving continuing treatment by a health care provider includes any one or more of the following:

Incapacity and Treatment

A period of incapacity of more than three consecutive, full calendar days, and any subsequent treatment or period of incapacity relating to the same condition, that also involves: a) treatment two or more times, within

30 days of the first day of incapacity, unless extenuating circumstances exist, by a health care provider, by a nurse under direct supervision of a health care provider, or by a provider of health care services (such as a physical therapist) under orders of, or on referral by, a health care provider, or b) treatment by a health care provider on at least one occasion, which results in a regimen of continuing treatment under the supervision of the health care provider. Treatment by a health care provider means that an in-patient visit to a health care provider and the first in-patient treatment visit must take place within seven days of the first day of incapacity. The necessity of additional treatment visits within the 30 day period or a regimen of continuing treatment is to be determined by the health care provider. Extenuating circumstances means circumstances beyond the employee's control that prevent the follow-up visit from occurring as planned by the health care provider. This may occur, for example, when the second in-person visit is needed within the 30 day period, but the health care provider does not have available appointments during that time period.

Pregnancy or Prenatal Care

Continuing treatment also includes any period of incapacity due to pregnancy or prenatal care. Absences attributable to incapacity for these reasons qualify for FMLA leave even though the employee or the covered family member does not receive treatment from a health care provider during the absence, and even if the absence does not last more than three consecutive, full calendar days. For example, an employee who is pregnant may be unable to report to work because of severe morning sickness.

Chronic Conditions

Incapacity or treatment may also result from chronic conditions. These are health conditions which, a) requires periodic visits (at least twice a year) for treatment by a health care provider, or by a nurse under direct supervision of a health care provider, b) continue over an extended period of time (including recurring episodes of a single underlying condition), and, c) may cause episodic rather than a continuing period of incapacity (such as, for example, asthma, diabetes or epilepsy). Absences attributable to incapacity for these reasons qualify for FMLA leave even though the employee or the covered family member does not receive treatment from a health care provider during the absence, and even if the absence does not last more than three consecutive, full calendar days. For example, an employee with asthma may be unable to report for work due to the onset of an asthma attack or because the employee's health care provider has advised the employee to stay home when the pollen count exceeds a certain level.

Permanent or Long-Term Conditions

At times, treatment may not be effective and an individual may still be incapacitated. The employee or family member must be under the continuing supervision of, but need not be receiving active treatment by, a health care provider. Some examples of these types of conditions could include Alzheimer's disease, a severe stroke, or the terminal stages of a disease.

Conditions That Require Multiple Treatments

These conditions include any period of absence to receive multiple treatments (including any period of recovery) by a health care provider or by a provider of health care services under orders of, or on referral by, a health care provider, for, a) restorative surgery after an accident or other injury, or, b) a condition that would likely result in a period of incapacity of more than three consecutive, full calendar days in the absence of medical intervention or treatment, such as, for example, cancer treatments (including chemotherapy and radiation), treatment for severe arthritis such as physical therapy, or kidney dialysis for kidney disease.

Family Members

Spouse

A husband or wife as defined or recognized under State law for purposes of marriage in the State where the employee resides, including common law marriage in States where it is recognized.

Parent

A biological, adoptive, step or foster father or mother, or any other individual who stood in loco parentis to the employee when the employee was a son or daughter. This term does not include parents "in law." Persons who are "in loco parentis" include those with day-to-day responsibilities to care for and financially support a child, or, in the case of an employee, who had such responsibility for the employee when the employee was a child. A biological or legal relationship is not necessary.

Son or Daughter

For purposes of FMLA leave taken for birth or adoption, or to care for a family member with a serious health condition, son or daughter means a biological, adopted, or foster child, a stepchild, a legal ward, or a child of a person standing in loco parentis, who is either under age 18, or age 18 or older and "incapable of self-care because of a mental or physical disability" at the time that FMLA leave is to commence.

Next of Kin of a Covered Servicemember

The nearest blood relative other than the covered servicemember's spouse, parent, son, or daughter, in the following order of priority: blood relatives who have been granted legal custody of the covered servicemember by court decree or statutory provisions, brothers and sisters, grandparents, aunts and uncles, and first cousins, unless the covered servicemember has specifically designated in writing another blood relative as his or her nearest blood relative for purposes of military caregiver leave under the FMLA. When no such designation is made, and there are multiple family members with the same level of relationship to the covered servicemember, all of these family members may be considered the covered servicemember's next of kin and may take FMLA leave to provide care to the covered servicemember, either consecutively or simultaneously. When such designation has been made, the designated individual shall be deemed to be the covered servicemember's only next of kin.

Adoption

Legally and permanently assuming the responsibility of raising a child as one's own. The source of an adopted child is not a factor in determining eligibility for FMLA leave.

Foster Care

Twenty four-hour care for children in substitution for, and away from, their parents or guardian. Such placement is made by or with the agreement of the State as a result of a voluntary agreement between the parent or guardian that the child be removed from the home, or pursuant to a judicial determination of the necessity for foster care, and involves agreement between the State and foster family that the foster family will take care of the child. Although foster care may be with relatives of the child, State action is generally involved in the removal of the child from parental custody.

Son or Daughter on Active Duty or Call to Active Duty Status

The employee's biological, adopted, or foster child, stepchild, legal ward, or a child for whom the employee stood in loco parentis, who is on active duty or call to active duty status, and who is of any age.

Son or Daughter of a Covered Servicemember

The servicemember's biological, adopted, or foster child, stepchild, legal ward, or a child for whom the servicemember stood in loco parentis, and who is of any age.

Parent of a Covered Servicemember

A covered servicemember's biological, adoptive, step or foster father or mother, or any other individual who stood in loco parentis to the covered servicemember. This term does not include parents "in law."

For purposes of confirmation of family relationship, the employer may require the employee giving notice of the need for leave to provide reasonable documentation or statement of family relationship. This documentation may take the form, for example, of a simple statement from the employee, or a child's birth certificate or a court document. The employer is entitled to examine the documentation provided but the employee is entitled to the return of the official document submitted for this purpose.

Unable to Perform the Functions of the Position

An employee is "unable to perform the functions of the position" where the health care provider finds that the employee is unable to work at all or is unable to perform any one of the essential functions of the employee's position as defined by the same definitions contained in the Americans with Disabilities Act (ADA), as amended. An employee who must be absent from work to receive medical treatment for a serious health condition is considered to be unable to perform the essential functions of the position during the absence for treatment.

Statement of Functions

An employer has the option, in requiring certification from a health care provider, to provide a statement of the essential functions of the employee's position for the health care provider to review. A sufficient medical certification must specify what functions of the employee's position the employee is unable to perform so that the employer can then determine whether the employee is unable to perform one or more essential functions of the employee's position. For purposes of the FMLA, the essential functions of the employee's position are to be determined with reference to the position the employee held at the time notice is given or leave commenced, whichever is earlier.

Needed to Care for a Family Member or Covered Servicemember

The medical certification provision that an employee is "needed to care for" a family member or covered servicemember encompasses both physical *and* psychological care. It includes situations where, for example, because of a serious health condition, the family member is unable to care for his or her own basic medical, hygienic, nutritional or safety needs, or is unable to transport himself or herself to the doctor. The term also includes providing psychological comfort and reassurance which would be beneficial to a child, spouse or parent with a serious health condition who is receiving inpatient or home care. It also includes situations where the employee may be needed to substitute for others who normally care for the family member or covered servicemember, or to make arrangements for changes in care, such as transfer to a nursing home. The employee need not be

66

the only individual or family member available to care for the family member or covered servicemember.

An employee's intermittent leave or a reduced schedule leave necessary to care for a family member or covered servicemember includes not only a situation where the condition of the family member or covered servicemember itself is intermittent, but also where the employee is only needed intermittently, such as where other care is normally available, or care responsibilities are shared with another member of the family or a third party.

Health Care Provider

The FMLA "health care provider" includes a doctor of medicine or osteopathy who is authorized to practice (which means authorized to diagnose and treat physical or mental health conditions) medicine or surgery (as appropriate) by the State in which the doctor practices. The statute permits the Secretary of Labor to make determinations of others who are capable of providing health care services. Those others include only a) podiatrists, dentists, clinical psychologists, optometrists, chiropractors (limited to treatment consisting of manual manipulation of the spine to correct a subluxation as demonstrated by X-ray to exist) authorized to practice in the State and performing within the scope of their practice as defined under State law; b) nurse practitioners, nurse midwives, clinical social workers and physician assistants who are authorized to practice under State law and who are performing within the scope of their practice as defined under State law; c) Christian Science practitioners listed with the First Church of Christ, Scientist in Boston, Massachusetts. Where an employee or family member is receiving treatment from a Christian Science practitioner, an employee may not object to any requirement from an employer that the employee or family member submit to examination (though not treatment) to obtain a second or third certification from a health care provider other than a Christian Science practitioner except as otherwise provided under applicable State or local law or collective bargaining agreement; d) any health care provider from whom an employer or the employer's group health plan's benefits manager will accept certification of the existence of a serious health condition to substantiate a claim for benefits; and e) a health care provider listed above who practices in a country other than the United States, who is authorized to practice in accordance with the law of that country, and who is performing within the scope of his or her practice as defined under such law.

Other Terms

Incapable of Self-Care

An individual requires active assistance or supervision to provide daily self-care in three or more of the "activities of daily living" (ADLs) or "instrumental activities of daily living" (IADLs). Activities of daily living include adaptive activities such as caring appropriately for one's grooming, hygiene, bathing, dressing and eating. Instrumental activities of daily living include cooking, cleaning, shopping, taking public transportation, paying bills, maintaining a residence, using telephones and directories, using a post office, etc.

Physical or Mental Disability

A physical or mental impairment that substantially limits one or more of the major life activities of an individual. The FMLA uses the same definitions that are used by the Americans With Disabilities Act to define these terms in more detail.

2

Leave Entitlements

Amount of Leave

An eligible employee's FMLA leave entitlement is limited to a total of 12 workweeks of leave during any 12-month period (except in the case of leave to care for a covered servicemember with a serious injury or illness) for any one, or more, of the following reasons, a) the birth of the employee's son or daughter, and to care for the newborn child, b) the placement with the employee of a son or daughter for adoption or foster care, and to care for the newly placed child, c) to care for the employee's spouse, son, daughter, or parent with a serious health condition, d) because of a serious health condition that makes the employee unable to perform one or more of the essential functions of his or her job, and e) because of any qualifying exigency arising out of the fact that the employee's spouse, son, daughter, or parent is a covered military member on active duty (or has been notified of an impending call or order to active duty) in support of a contingency operation.

The employer is permitted to choose any one of the following methods for determining the 12-month period in which the 12 weeks of leave entitlement occurs, a) the calendar year, b) any fixed 12-month leave year, such as a fiscal year, a year required by State law, or a year starting on an employee's anniversary date, c) the 12-month period measured forward from the date any employee's first FMLA leave begins ("rolling forward"), or d) a "rolling" 12-month period measured backward from the date an employee uses any FMLA leave ("rolling backward").

If the employer selects the calendar or fixed 12-month year, an employee would be entitled to up to 12 weeks of FMLA leave at any time in the fixed 12-month period selected. An employee could, therefore, take 12 weeks of leave at the end of the year and 12 weeks at the beginning of the following year. If the employer chose the rolling forward method, an employee would be entitled to 12 weeks of leave during the year beginning on the first date FMLA leave is taken; the next 12-month period would begin the first time FMLA leave is taken after completion of any previous 12-month period.

Under the rolling backward method, each time an employee takes FMLA leave the remaining leave entitlement would be any balance of the 12 weeks which has not been used during the immediately preceding 12 months. The regulations provide the following example to illustrate this point: if an employee has taken eight weeks of leave during the past 12 months, an additional four weeks of leave could be taken. If an employee used four weeks beginning February 1, 2008, four weeks beginning June 1, 2008, and four weeks beginning December 1, 2008, the employee would not be entitled to any additional leave until February 1, 2009. However, beginning on February 1, 2009, the employee would again be eligible to take FMLA leave, recouping the right to take the leave in the same manner and amounts in which it was used in the previous year. Thus, the employee would recoup (and be entitled to use) one additional day of FMLA leave each day for four weeks, commencing February 1, 2009. The employee would also begin to recoup additional days beginning on June 1, 2009, and additional days beginning on December 1, 2009. Accordingly, employers using the rolling 12-month period may need to calculate whether the employee is entitled to take FMLA leave each time that leave is requested, and employees taking FMLA leave on such a basis may fall in and out of FMLA protection based on their FMLA usage in the prior 12 months. For example, in the example above, if the employee needs six weeks of leave for a serious health condition commencing February 1, 2009, only the first four weeks of the leave would be FMLA-protected.

Employers are permitted to choose any one of the four methods described above for calculating the 12-month period, as long as it is applied consistently and uniformly to all employees. If the employer wishes to change from one method to another, it is required to give at least 60 days notice to all employees, and the transition must take place in such a way that the employees retain the full benefit of 12 weeks of leave under whichever method affords the greatest benefit to the employee. The only exception to the requirement of uniform application of the 12-month period occurs when a multistate employer has employees in a state which requires a certain method of determining the 12-month period.

When such a method conflicts with the method chosen by the employer to determine the 12-month period under the FMLA, the employer may comply with the State law for the employees who are employed in that state and uniformly use one of the other methods permissible under the FMLA for all other employees.

Employers should be aware that if they do not select, as a matter of policy, one of the four permissible methods of calculating the 12-month period their policies are unclear as how they intend to calculate the 12-month period, the option that provides the most beneficial outcome for the employee will be used. Once the employer realizes the error of its ways, the employer may subsequently select an option only by providing the 60-day notice to all employees of the option the employer intends to implement. During the running of the 60-day period any other employee who needs FMLA leave may use the option providing the most beneficial outcome to that employee. At the conclusion of the 60-day period the employer may implement the selected option.

As a reminder, an eligible employee's FMLA leave entitlement is limited to a total of 26 workweeks of leave during a single 12-month period to care for a covered servicemember with a serious injury or illness. An employer is required to use the rolling forward method described above for calculating the leave. And, during the single 12-month period, an eligible employee's FMLA leave entitlement is limited to a combined total of 26 workweeks of FMLA leave for any qualifying reason.

A holiday that occurs within a week taken as FMLA leave has no effect. In other words, the week is counted as a week of FMLA leave. However, if an employee is using FMLA leave in increments of less than one week, the holiday will not count against the employee's FMLA entitlement unless the employee was otherwise scheduled and expected to work during the holiday. Similarly, if for some reason the employer's business activity has temporarily ceased and employees generally are not expected to report for work for one or more weeks (such as a school closing two weeks for the Christmas/New Year holiday or the summer vacation or an employer closing the plant for retooling or repairs), the days the employer's activities have ceased do not count against the employee's FMLA leave entitlement.

Intermittent Leave

Intermittent Leave or Reduced Schedule Leave

Intermittent leave is FMLA leave taken in separate blocks of time due to a single qualifying reason. A reduced schedule leave is a leave schedule that reduces an employee's usual number of working hours per workweek or hours per workday. A reduced schedule leave is a change in the employee's schedule for a period of time, normally from full-time to part-time.

For intermittent leave or leave on a reduced schedule leave taken because of one's own serious health condition, to care for a parent, son, or daughter with a serious health condition, or to care for a covered servicemember with a serious injury or illness, there must be a medical need for leave and it must be demonstrated that such medical need can be best accommodated through an intermittent or reduced schedule leave. The treatment regimen and other information described in the certification of a serious health condition and in the certification of a serious injury or illness, if required by the employer, addresses the medical necessity of intermittent leave or leave on a reduced schedule leave.

Leave may be taken intermittently or on a reduced schedule leave when medically necessary for planned and/or unanticipated medical treatment of a serious health condition or of a covered servicemember's serious injury or illness, or for recovery from treatment or recovery from a serious health condition or a covered servicemember's serious injury or illness. It may also be taken to provide care or psychological comfort to a covered family member with a serious health condition or a covered servicemember with a serious injury or illness.

Intermittent leave may be taken for a serious health condition of a parent, son, or daughter, for the employee's own serious health condition, or a serious injury or illness of a covered servicemember which requires treatment by a health care provider periodically, rather than for one continuous period of time, and may include leave of periods from an hour or more to several weeks. Examples of intermittent leave would include leave taken on an occasional basis for medical appointments, or leave taken several days at a time spread over a period of six months, such as for chemotherapy. A pregnant employee may take leave intermittently for prenatal examinations or for her own condition, such as for periods of severe morning sickness. An example of an employee taking leave on a reduced schedule leave is an employee who is recovering from a serious health condition and is not strong enough to work a full-time schedule.

Intermittent or reduced schedule leave may be taken for absences where the employee or family member is incapacitated or unable to perform the essential functions of the position because of a chronic serious health condition or a serious injury or illness of a covered servicemember, even if he or she does not receive treatment by a health care provider.

The rules for birth or placement differ slightly. When leave is taken after the birth of a healthy child or placement of a healthy child for adoption or foster care, an employee may take leave intermittently or on a reduced schedule leave only if the employer agrees. Such a schedule reduction might occur, for example, where an employee, with the employer's agreement, works part-time after the birth of a child, or takes leave in several segments. The employer's agreement is not required, however, for leave during which the mother has a serious health condition in connection with the birth of her child or if the newborn child has a serious health condition.

Scheduling of Intermittent or Reduced Schedule Leave

Employees may take FMLA leave on an intermittent or reduced schedule basis when medically necessary due to the serious health condition of a covered family member or the employee or the serious injury or illness of a covered servicemember. Employees may also take FMLA leave on an intermittent or reduced schedule basis when necessary because of a qualifying exigency. If an employee needs leave intermittently or on a reduced schedule leave for planned medical treatment, then the employee must make a reasonable effort to schedule the treatment so as not to disrupt unduly the employer's operations.

Transfer of an Employee to an Alternative Position During Intermittent Leave or Reduced Schedule Leave

If an employee needs intermittent leave or leave on a reduced schedule leave that is foreseeable based on planned medical treatment for the employee, a family member, or a covered servicemember, including during a period of recovery from one's own serious health condition, a serious health condition of a spouse, parent, son, or daughter, or a serious injury or illness of a covered servicemember, or if the employer agrees to permit intermittent or reduced schedule leave for the birth of a child or for placement of a child for adoption or foster care, the employer may require the employee to transfer temporarily, during the period that the intermittent or reduced schedule leave is required, to an available alternative position for which the employee is qualified and which better accommodates recurring periods of leave than does the employee's regular position.

Transfer to an alternative position may require compliance with any applicable collective bargaining agreement, Federal law (such as the Americans with Disabilities Act), and State law. Transfer to an alternative position may include altering an existing job to better accommodate the employee's need for intermittent or reduced schedule leave. In addition, the alternative position must have equivalent pay and benefits. An alternative position for these purposes does not have to have equivalent duties. The employer may increase the pay and benefits of an existing alternative position, so as to make them equivalent to the pay and benefits of the employee's regular job. The employer may also transfer the employee to a part-time job with the same hourly rate of pay and benefits, provided the employee is not required to take more leave than is medically necessary. For example, an employee desiring to take leave in increments of four hours per day could be transferred to a half-time job, or could remain in the employee's same job on a part-time schedule, paying the same hourly rate as the employee's previous job and enjoying the same benefits. The employer may not eliminate benefits which otherwise would not be provided to part-time employees; however, an employer may proportionately reduce benefits such as vacation leave where an employer's normal practice is to base such benefits on the number of hours worked.

An employer is prohibited from transferring the employee to an alternative position in order to discourage the employee from taking leave or otherwise creating a hardship for the employee. The Regulations provide the following examples to illustrate this point: a white collar employee may not be assigned to perform laborer's work; an employee working the day shift may not be reassigned to the graveyard shift; an employee working in the headquarters facility may not be reassigned to a branch a significant distance away from the employee's normal job location.

When an employee who is taking leave intermittently or on a reduced schedule leave and has been transferred to an alternative position no longer needs to continue on leave and is able to return to full-time work, the employee must be placed in the same or equivalent job as the job he or she left when the leave commenced. An employee may not be required to take more leave than necessary to address the circumstance that precipitated the need for leave.

Increments and Calculation of FMLA Leave for Intermittent or Reduced Schedule Leave

When an employee takes FMLA leave on an intermittent or reduced schedule leave basis, the employer must account for the leave using an increment no greater than the shortest period of time that the employer uses to account for use of other forms of leave provided that it is not greater than one hour and provided further that an employee's FMLA leave entitlement may not be reduced by more than the amount of leave actually taken. If an employer accounts for use of leave in varying increments at different times of the day or shift, the employer may not account for FMLA leave in a larger increment than the shortest period used to account for other leave during the period in which the FMLA leave is taken. If an employer accounts for other forms of leave use in increments greater than one hour, the employer must account for FMLA leave use in increments no greater than one hour. An employer may account for FMLA leave in shorter increments than used for other forms of leave. For example, an employer that accounts for other forms of leave in one hour increments may account for FMLA leave in a shorter increment when the employee arrives at work several minutes late, and the employer wants the employee to begin work immediately. Such accounting for FMLA leave will not alter the increment considered to be the shortest period used to account for other forms of leave or the use of FMLA leave in other circumstances.

Where it is physically impossible for an employee using intermittent leave or working a reduced schedule leave to commence or end work mid-way through a shift, such as for example, where a flight attendant or a railroad conductor is scheduled to work aboard an airplane or train, or a laboratory employee is unable to enter or leave a sealed clean room during a certain period of time, the entire period that the employee is forced to be absent is designated as FMLA leave and counts against the employee's FMLA entitlement.

When an employee takes leave on an intermittent or reduced schedule leave, only the amount of leave actually taken may be counted toward the employee's leave entitlement. The actual workweek is the basis of leave entitlement. Therefore, if an employee who would otherwise work 40 hours a week takes off 8 hours, the employee would have used one fifth of a week of FMLA leave. Similarly, if a full-time employee who would otherwise work 8-hour days works 4-hour days under a reduced schedule leave, the employee would have used one half of a week of FMLA leave. Where an employee works a part-time schedule or variable hours, the amount of FMLA leave that an employee uses is determined on a pro rata or proportional basis. For example, if an employee who would otherwise work 30 hours per week, but works only 20 hours a week under a reduced schedule leave, the employee's ten hours of leave would constitute one-third (1/3) of a week of FMLA leave for each week the employee works the reduced schedule leave. An employer is permitted to convert these fractions to their hourly equivalent so long as the conversion equitably reflects the employee's total normally scheduled hours. If an employee's schedule varies from week to week to such an extent that an employer is unable to determine with any certainty how many hours the employee would otherwise have worked (but for the taking of FMLA leave), a weekly average of the hours scheduled over the 12 months prior to the beginning of the leave period (including any hours for which the employee took leave of any type) would be used for calculating the employee's leave entitlement. If, for reasons other than FMLA, and prior to the notice of need for FMLA leave, an employer has made a permanent or long-term change in the employee's schedule, the hours worked under the new schedule are to be used for making this calculation.

If an employee would normally be required to work overtime, but is unable to do so because of a FMLA-qualifying reason that limits the employee's ability to work overtime, the hours which the employee would have been required to work may be counted against the employee's FMLA entitlement. In such a case, the employee is using intermittent or reduced schedule leave. For example, if an employee would normally be required to work for 48 hours in a particular week, but due to a serious health condition the employee is unable to work more than 40 hours that week, the employee would utilize eight hours of FMLA-protected leave out of the 48-hour workweek (8/48 = 1/6 workweek). Voluntary overtime hours that an employee does not work due to a serious health condition may not be counted against the employee's FMLA leave entitlement.

Interaction of the FMLA with the FLSA

Leave taken under FMLA may be unpaid. If an employee is otherwise exempt from the minimum wage and overtime requirements of the Fair Labor Standards Act (FLSA) as a salaried executive, administrative, professional, or computer professional, providing unpaid FMLA leave to such an employee will <u>not</u> cause the employee to lose their FLSA exemption. This means that under regulations currently in effect, where an employee meets the specified duties test, is paid on a salary basis, and is paid a salary of at least the amount specified in the regulations, the employer may make deductions from the employee's salary for any hours taken as intermittent or reduced FMLA leave within a workweek, without affecting the exempt status of the employee. The fact that an employer provides FMLA leave, whether paid or unpaid, and maintains records regarding FMLA leave, will not be relevant to the determination whether an employee is exempt under the FLSA. Deductions may not be taken from such an employee's salary for any leave which does not qualify as FMLA leave, for example, deductions from an employee's pay for leave required under State law or under an employer's policy or practice for a reason which does not qualify as FMLA leave.

If an employee is paid in accordance with the fluctuating workweek method of payment for overtime under the FLSA, the employer, during the period in which intermittent or reduced schedule FMLA leave is scheduled to be taken, may compensate an employee on an hourly basis and pay only for the hours the employee works (including time and one-half the employee's regular rate for overtime hours). The change to payment on an hourly basis would include the entire period during which the employee is taking intermittent leave, including weeks in which no leave is taken. The hourly rate is determined by dividing the employee's weekly salary by the employee's normal or average schedule of hours worked during weeks in which FMLA leave is not being taken. If an employer chooses to follow this exception from the fluctuating workweek method of payment, the employer must do so uniformly, with respect to all employees paid on a fluctuating workweek basis for whom FMLA leave is taken on an intermittent or reduced schedule leave basis. If an employer does not elect to convert the employee's compensation to hourly pay, no deduction may be taken for FMLA leave absences. Once the need for intermittent or reduced scheduled leave is over, the employee may be restored to payment on a fluctuating work week basis.

Employee Benefits

Substitution of Paid Leave

The FMLA permits an eligible employee to choose to substitute accrued paid leave for FMLA leave. If an employee does not choose to substitute accrued paid leave, the employer may require the employee to substitute accrued paid leave for unpaid FMLA leave. The term "substitute" means that the paid leave provided by the employer, and accrued pursuant to established policies of the employer, will run concurrently with the unpaid FMLA leave. Accordingly, the employee receives pay pursuant to the employer's applicable paid leave policy during the period of otherwise unpaid FMLA leave. An employee's ability to substitute accrued paid leave is determined by the terms and conditions of the employer's normal leave policy. When an employee chooses, or an employer requires, substitution of accrued paid leave, the employer must inform the employee that the employee must satisfy any procedural requirements of the paid leave policy only in connection with the receipt of such payment. If an employee does not comply with the additional requirements in an employer's paid leave policy, the employee is not entitled to substitute accrued paid leave, but the employee remains entitled to take unpaid FMLA leave. If neither the employee nor the employer elects to substitute paid leave for unpaid FMLA leave under the above conditions and circumstances, the employee will remain entitled to all the paid leave which is earned or accrued under the terms of the employer's plan. Employers may not discriminate against employees on FMLA leave in the administration of their paid leave policies.

If an employee uses paid leave under circumstances which do not qualify as FMLA leave, the leave will not count against the employee's FMLA leave entitlement. For example, paid sick leave used for a medical condition which is not a serious health condition or serious injury or illness does not count against the employee's FMLA leave entitlement. Leave taken pursuant to a disability leave plan would generally be considered FMLA leave for a serious health condition and counted in the leave entitlement permitted under the FMLA. In such cases, the employer may designate the leave as FMLA leave and count the leave against the employee's FMLA leave entitlement. Because leave pursuant to a disability benefit plan is not unpaid, the provision for substitution of the employee's accrued paid leave is inapplicable, and neither the employee nor the employer may require the substitution of paid leave. However, employers and employees may agree, where State law permits, to have paid leave supplement the disability plan benefits, such as in the case where a plan only provides replacement income for two thirds of pay.

The Act provides that a serious health condition may result from injury to the employee on or off the job. If the employer designates the leave as FMLA leave, the leave counts against the employee's FMLA leave entitlement. Because the workers' compensation absence is not unpaid, the provision for substitution of the employee's accrued paid leave is not applicable, and neither the employee nor the employer may require the substitution of paid leave. However, employers and employees may agree, where State law permits, to have paid leave supplement workers' compensation benefits, such as in the case where workers' compensation only provides replacement income for two thirds of an employee's salary. If the health care provider treating the employee for the workers' compensation injury certifies the employee is able to return to a light duty job but is unable to return to the same or equivalent job, the employee may decline the employer's offer of a light duty job. As a result the employee may lose workers' compensation payments, but is entitled to remain on unpaid FMLA leave until the employee's FMLA leave entitlement is exhausted. As of the date workers' compensation benefits cease, the substitution provision becomes applicable and either the employee may elect or the employer may require the use of accrued paid leave.

Maintenance of Employee Benefits

During any FMLA leave, an employer must maintain the employee's coverage under any group health plan on the same conditions as coverage would have been provided if the employee had been continuously employed during the entire leave period. All employers covered by FMLA, including public agencies, are subject to the Act's requirements to maintain health coverage.

A group health plan under the FMLA is a plan of an employer or contributed to by an employer (including a self-insured plan) to provide health care (directly or otherwise) to the employer's employees, former employees, or the families of such employees or former employees. It does not include an insurance program providing health coverage under which employees purchase individual policies from insurers provided that, a) no contributions are made by the employer, b) participation in the program is completely voluntary for employ-

ees, c) the sole functions of the employer with respect
to the program are, without endorsing the program, to
permit the insurer to publicize the program to employees, to collect premiums through payroll deductions
and to remit them to the insurer, d) the employer receives no consideration in the form of cash or otherwise
in connection with the program, other than reasonable
compensation, excluding any profit, for administrative
services actually rendered in connection with payroll
deduction, and e) the premium charged with respect to
such coverage does not increase in the event the employment relationship terminates.

During his leave, the employee is entitled to the same
group health plan benefits he had prior to taking FMLA
leave. For example, if family member coverage is provided to an employee, family member coverage must be
maintained during the FMLA leave. Similarly, benefit
coverage during FMLA leave for medical care, surgical
care, hospital care, dental care, eye care, mental health
counseling, substance abuse treatment, etc., must be
maintained during leave if provided in an employer's
group health plan, including a supplement to a group
health plan, whether or not provided through a flex-
ible spending account or other component of a cafeteria
plan.

If an employer provides a new health plan or benefits or
changes health benefits or plans while an employee is
on FMLA leave, the employee is entitled to the new or
changed plan/benefits to the same extent as if the employee were not on leave. For example, if an employer
changes a group health plan so that dental care becomes
covered under the plan, an employee on FMLA leave

must be given the same opportunity as other employees to receive (or obtain) the dental care coverage. Any other plan changes (such as, for example, in coverage, premiums, deductibles, etc.) which apply to all employees of the workforce would also apply to an employee on FMLA leave.

Notice of any opportunity to change plans or benefits must also be given to an employee on FMLA leave. If the group health plan permits an employee to change from single to family coverage upon the birth of a child or otherwise add new family members, such a change in benefits must be made available while an employee is on FMLA leave. If the employee requests the changed coverage it must be provided by the employer.

An employee may choose not to retain group health plan coverage during FMLA leave. However, when an employee returns from leave, the employee is entitled to be reinstated on the same terms as prior to taking the leave, including family or dependent coverages, without any qualifying period, physical examination, or exclusion of pre-existing conditions.

Except as required by the Consolidated Omnibus Budget Reconciliation Act of 1986 (COBRA) and for "key" employees (as discussed elsewhere in this guide), an employer's obligation to maintain health benefits during leave (and to restore the employee to the same or equivalent employment) under FMLA terminates under the following circumstances, a) if and when the employment relationship would have terminated if the employee had not taken FMLA leave (i.e., if the employee's position is eliminated as part of a lawful reduction in force and the employee would not have been transferred to another position), b) an employee informs the employer of his or her intent not to return from leave (including before starting the leave if the employer is so informed before the leave starts), or, c) the employee fails to return from leave or continues on leave after exhausting his or her FMLA leave entitlement in the 12-month period.

If a key employee does not return from leave when notified by the employer that substantial or grievous economic injury will result from his or her reinstatement, the employee's entitlement to group health plan benefits continues unless and until the employee advises the employer that the employee does not desire restoration to employment at the end of the leave period, or the FMLA leave entitlement is exhausted, or reinstatement is actually denied.

An employee's entitlement to benefits other than group health benefits during a period of FMLA leave (such as, for example, holiday pay) is to be determined by the employer's established policy for providing such benefits when the employee is on other forms of leave (paid or unpaid, as appropriate).

Employee Payment of Group Health Benefit Premiums

Group health plan benefits must be maintained on the same basis as coverage would have been provided if the employee had been continuously employed during the FMLA leave period. Therefore, any share of group health plan premiums which had been paid by the employee prior to FMLA leave must continue to be paid by the employee during the FMLA leave period. If premiums are raised or lowered, the employee would be required to pay the new premium rates. Maintenance of health insurance policies which are not a part of the employer's group health plan, are the sole responsibility of the employee. The employee and the insurer should make necessary arrangements for payment of premiums during periods of unpaid FMLA leave.

Generally, if the FMLA leave is substituted with paid leave, the employee's share of premiums must be paid by the method normally used during any paid leave, presumably as a payroll deduction. However, if the FMLA leave is unpaid, the employer has a number of options for obtaining payment from the employee. The employer may require that payment be made to the employer or to the insurance carrier, but no additional charge may be added to the employee's premium payment for administrative expenses. The employer must provide the employee with advance written notice of the terms and conditions under which these payments must be made.

The employer may require employees to pay their share of premium payments in any of the following ways, a) payment would be due at the same time as it would be made if by payroll deduction, b) payment would be due on the same schedule as payments are made under COBRA (but remember FMLA leave is not a qualifying event under COBRA), c) payment would be prepaid pursuant to a cafeteria plan at the employee's option, d) the employer's existing rules for payment by employees on "leave without pay" would be followed, so long as these rules do not require prepayment, prior to the commencement of the leave, of the premiums that will become due during a period of unpaid FMLA leave or payment of higher premiums than if the employee had continued to work instead of taking leave, or, e) another system voluntarily agreed to between the employer and the employee, which may include, for example, prepayment of premiums through increased payroll deductions when the need for the FMLA leave is foreseeable. With respect to "leave without pay," specifically, an employer may not require more of an employee using unpaid FMLA leave than the employer requires of other employees on "leave without pay."

An employee who is receiving payments as a result of a workers' compensation injury must make arrangements with the employer for payment of group health plan benefits when simultaneously taking FMLA leave.

Maintenance of Benefits under Multi-Employer Health Plans

A multi-employer health plan is a plan to which more than one employer is required to contribute, and which is maintained pursuant to one or more collective bargaining agreements between employee organization(s) and the employers. An employer under a multi-employer plan must continue to make contributions on behalf of an employee using FMLA leave as though the employee had been continuously employed, unless the plan contains an explicit FMLA provision for maintaining coverage such as through pooled contributions by all employers participating in the plan.

During the duration of an employee's FMLA leave, coverage by the group health plan, and benefits provided pursuant to the plan, must be maintained at the level of coverage and benefits which were applicable to the employee at the time FMLA leave commenced.

An employee using FMLA leave cannot be required to use "banked" hours or pay a greater premium than the employee would have been required to pay if the employee had been continuously employed.

Group health plan coverage must be maintained for an employee on FMLA leave until, a) the employee's FMLA leave entitlement is exhausted, b) the employer can show that the employee would have been laid off and the employment relationship terminated, or, c) the employee provides unequivocal notice of intent not to return to work.

Employee Failure to Pay Health Plan Premium Payments

An employer's obligations to maintain health insurance coverage cease under FMLA if an employee's premium payment is more than 30 days late. The employer, however, is permitted to establish a longer grace period. In order to drop the coverage for an employee whose premium payment is late the following procedure must be followed, a), the employer must provide written notice to the employee that the payment has not been received, and, b) such notice must be mailed to the employee at least 15 days before coverage is to cease, advising that coverage will be dropped on a specified date at least 15 days after the date of the letter unless the payment has been received by that date. If the employer has established policies regarding other forms of unpaid leave that provide for the employer to cease coverage retroactively to the date the unpaid premium payment was due, the employer may drop the employee from coverage retroactively in accordance with that policy, provided the 15-day notice was given. In the absence of such a policy, coverage for the employee may be terminated at the end of the 30-day grace period, where the required 15-day notice has been provided. An employer has no obligation regarding the maintenance of a health insurance policy which is not a group health plan (as defined elsewhere in this guide). Failure of an employer to pay his/her health plan premiums does not impact the employer continued obligation to reinstate the employee upon return from leave.

The employer may recover the employee's share of any premium payments missed by the employee for any FMLA leave period during which the employer maintained that employee's health coverage by paying the employee's portion of the premium that the employee failed to pay.

If coverage lapses because an employee has not made required premium payments, upon the employee's return from FMLA leave, the employer must still restore the employee to coverage/benefits equivalent to those the employee would have had if leave had not been taken and the premium payment(s) had not been missed (including family or dependent coverage). In such instances, an employee may not be required to meet any qualification requirements imposed by the plan, including any new preexisting condition waiting period, to wait for an open season, or to pass a medical examination to obtain reinstatement of coverage. If an employer terminates an employee's insurance in accordance with this section and fails to restore the employee's health insurance as required by this section upon the employee's return, the employer may be liable for benefits lost by reason of the violation, for other actual monetary losses sustained as a direct result of the violation, and for appropriate equitable relief tailored to the harm suffered.

Employer Recovery of Benefit Costs

An employer may recover its share of health plan premiums during a period of unpaid FMLA leave from an employee if the employee fails to return to work after the employee's FMLA leave entitlement has been exhausted or expires, unless the reason the employee does not return is due to, a) the continuation, recurrence, or onset of either a serious health condition of the employee or the employee's family member, or a serious injury or illness of a covered servicemember, which would otherwise entitle the employee to leave under FMLA, or, b) other circumstances beyond the employee's control.

The Regulations explain that the definition of "other circumstances beyond the employee's control" is intended to be broad. For example, such circumstances include situations as where a parent chooses to stay home with a newborn child who has a serious health condition; an employee's spouse is unexpectedly transferred to a job location more than 75 miles from the employee's worksite; a relative or individual other than a covered family member has a serious health condition and the employee is needed to provide care; the employee is laid off while on leave; or, the employee is a "key employee" who decides not to return to work upon being notified of the employer's intention to deny restoration because of substantial and grievous economic injury to the employer's operations and is not reinstated by the employer. Other circumstances beyond the employee's control would not include a situation where an employee desires to remain with a parent in a distant city even though the parent no longer requires the employee's care, or a parent chooses not to return to work to stay home with a well, newborn child.

When an employee fails to return to work because of the continuation, recurrence, or onset of either a serious health condition of the employee or employee's family member, or a serious injury or illness of a covered servicemember, thereby precluding the employer from recovering its share of health benefit premium payments made on the employee's behalf during a period of unpaid FMLA leave, the employer may require medical certification of the employee's or the family member's serious health condition or the covered servicemember's serious injury or illness. Such certification is not required unless requested by the employer. The cost of the certification is borne by the employee, and the employee is not entitled to be paid for the time or travel costs spent in acquiring the certification. The employee is required to provide medical certification in a timely manner, defined as being within 30 days from the date of the employer's request. For purposes of medical certification, the employee may use the optional forms developed for these by the United States Department of Labor. If the employer requests medical certification and the employee does not provide the certification in a timely manner (within 30 days), or the reason for not returning to work does not meet the test of other circumstances beyond the employee's control, the employer may recover 100% of the health benefit premiums it paid during the period of unpaid FMLA leave.

Under some circumstances an employer may elect to maintain other benefits (such as, for example, life insurance or disability insurance) by paying the employee's share of premiums during periods of unpaid FMLA leave. For example, to ensure the employer can meet its responsibilities to provide equivalent benefits to the employee upon return from unpaid FMLA leave, it may be necessary that premiums be paid continuously to avoid a lapse of coverage. If the employer elects to maintain such benefits during the leave, at the conclusion of leave, the employer is entitled to recover only the costs incurred for paying the employee's share of any premiums whether or not the employee returns to work. In addition, an employee who returns to work for at least 30 calendar days is considered to have returned to work. An employee who transfers directly from taking FMLA leave to retirement, or who retires during the first 30 days after the employee returns to work, is deemed to have returned to work.

When an employee elects or an employer requires paid leave to be substituted for FMLA leave, the employer may not recover its share of health insurance or other non-health benefit premiums for any period of FMLA leave covered by paid leave. Because paid leave provided under a plan covering temporary disabilities (including workers' compensation) is not unpaid, recovery of health insurance premiums does not apply to such paid leave.

The amount that self-insured employers may recover is limited to only the employer's share of allowable premiums as would be calculated under COBRA, excluding the 2 percent fee for administrative costs.

When an employee fails to return to work, any health and non-health benefit premiums which are permitted to be recovered under the FMLA, are a debt owed by the non-returning employee to the employer. The existence of this debt caused by the employee's failure to return to work does not alter the employer's responsibilities for health benefit coverage and, under a self-insurance plan, payment of claims incurred during the period of FMLA leave. To the extent recovery is allowed, the employer may recover the costs through deduction from any sums due to the employee. Employers are cautioned, however, to be sure that any deductions from unpaid wages, vacation pay, profit sharing plans, and the like are lawful under State or Federal wage payment laws. Alternatively, the employer may initiate legal action against the employee to recover such costs.

Reinstatement

Employee Right to Reinstatement

Upon return from FMLA leave, an employee is entitled to be returned to the same position the employee held when leave commenced, or to an equivalent position with equivalent benefits, pay, and other terms and conditions of employment. An employee is entitled to such reinstatement even if the employee has been replaced or his or her position has been restructured to accommodate the employee's absence.

Equivalent Position

An equivalent position is one that is virtually identical to the employee's former position in terms of pay, benefits and working conditions, including privileges, perquisites and status. It must have substantially similar duties, conditions, responsibilities, privileges and status as the employee's original position. It must involve the same or substantially similar duties and responsibilities, which must entail substantially equivalent skill, effort, responsibility, authority and the employee is ordinarily entitled to return to the same shift or the same or an equivalent work schedule.

If an employee is no longer qualified for the position because of, for example, the employee's inability to attend a necessary course or renew a license, as a result of the leave, the employee must be given a reasonable opportunity to fulfill those conditions upon his or her return to work.

The employee must be reinstated to the same or a geographically proximate worksite (one, for example, that does not involve a significant increase in commuting time or distance) from where the employee had previously been employed. If the employee's original worksite has been closed, the employee is entitled to the same rights as if the employee had not been on leave when the worksite closed. Thus, for example, if an employer transfers all employees from a closed worksite to a new worksite in a different city, the employee on leave is also entitled to transfer under the same conditions as if he or she had continued to be employed.

The FMLA does not prohibit an employer from accommodating an employee's request to be restored to a different shift, schedule, or position which better suits the employee's personal needs on return from leave, or to offer a promotion to a better position. However, an employee cannot be induced by the employer to accept a different position against the employee's wishes.

Equivalent Pay

The employee must have the same or an equivalent opportunity for bonuses, profit-sharing, and other similar discretionary and nondiscretionary payments. He/she is also entitled to any unconditional pay increases which may have occurred during the FMLA leave period, such as cost of living increases. Pay increases conditioned upon seniority, length of service, or work performed must be granted in accordance with the employer's policy or practice with respect to other employees on an equivalent leave status for a reason that does not qualify as FMLA leave. An employee is entitled to be restored to a position with the same or equivalent pay premiums, such as a shift differential. If an employee departed from a position averaging ten hours of overtime (and corresponding overtime pay) each week, an employee is ordinarily entitled to such a position on return from FMLA leave.

Equivalent pay includes any bonus or payment, whether it is discretionary or non-discretionary, made to employees. However, if a bonus or other payment is based on the achievement of a specified goal such as hours worked, products sold or perfect attendance, and the employee has not met the goal due to FMLA leave, then the payment may be denied, unless otherwise paid to employees on an equivalent leave status for a reason that does not qualify as FMLA leave. For example, if an employee who used paid vacation leave for a non-FMLA purpose would receive the payment, then the employee who used paid vacation leave for an FMLA protected purpose also must receive the payment.

Equivalent Benefits

With regard to equivalent benefits, benefits include all benefits provided or made available to employees by an employer, including group life insurance, health insurance, disability insurance, sick leave, annual leave, educational benefits, and pensions, regardless of whether such benefits are provided by a practice or written policy of an employer through an employee benefit plan (as defined by the Employee Retirement Income Security Act of 1974).

At the end of an employee's FMLA leave, benefits must be resumed in the same manner and at the same levels as provided when the leave began, and subject to any changes in benefit levels that may have taken place during the period of FMLA leave affecting the entire workforce, unless otherwise elected by the employee. Upon return from FMLA leave, an employee cannot be required to requalify for any benefits the employee enjoyed before FMLA leave began (including family or dependent coverages). For example, if an employee was covered by a life insurance policy before taking leave but is not covered or coverage lapses during the period of unpaid FMLA leave, the employee cannot be required to meet any qualifications, such as taking a physical examination, in order to requalify for life insurance upon return from leave. Accordingly, some employers may find it necessary to modify life insurance and other benefits programs in order to restore employees to equivalent benefits upon return from FMLA leave, make arrangements for continued payment of costs to maintain such benefits during unpaid FMLA leave, or pay these costs subject to recovery from the employee on return from leave.

An employee may, but is not entitled to, accrue any additional benefits or seniority during unpaid FMLA leave. Benefits accrued at the time leave began, however, (such as, for example, paid vacation, sick or personal leave to the extent not substituted for FMLA leave) must be available to an employee upon return from leave.

If, while on unpaid FMLA leave, an employee desires to continue life insurance, disability insurance, or other types of benefits for which he or she typically pays, the employer is required to follow established policies or practices for continuing such benefits for other instances of leave without pay. If the employer has no established policy, the employee and the employer are encouraged to agree upon arrangements before FMLA leave begins.

With respect to pension and other retirement plans, any period of unpaid FMLA leave may not be treated as or counted toward a break in service for purposes of vesting and eligibility to participate. Also, if the plan requires an employee to be employed on a specific date in order to be credited with a year of service for vesting, contributions or participation purposes, an employee on unpaid FMLA leave on that date shall be deemed to have been employed on that date. However, unpaid FMLA leave periods need not be treated as credited service for purposes of benefit accrual, vesting and eligibility to participate.

Employees on unpaid FMLA leave must be treated as if they continued to work for purposes of changes to benefit plans. They are entitled to changes in benefits plans, except those which may be dependent upon seniority or accrual during the leave period, immediately upon return from leave or to the same extent they would have qualified if no leave had been taken. For example, if the benefit plan is predicated on a preestablished number of hours worked each year and the employee does not have sufficient hours as a result of taking unpaid FMLA leave, the benefit is lost.

Limitations on an Employee's Right to Reinstatement

An employee has no greater right to reinstatement or to other benefits and conditions of employment than if the employee had been continuously employed during the FMLA leave period. An employer must be able to show that an employee would not otherwise have been employed at the time reinstatement is requested in order to deny restoration to employment. Thus, for example if an employee is laid off during the course of taking FMLA leave and employment is terminated, the employer's responsibility to continue FMLA leave, maintain group health plan benefits and restore the employee cease at the time the employee is laid off, provided the employer has no continuing obligations under a collective bargaining agreement or otherwise. An employer would have the burden of proving that an employee would have been laid off during the FMLA leave period and, therefore, would not be entitled to restoration.

If a shift has been eliminated, or overtime has been decreased, an employee would not be entitled to return to work that shift or the original overtime hours upon restoration. However, if, for example, a position on a night shift has been filled by another employee, the employee returning from FMLA leave is entitled to return to the same shift on which he/she was employed before taking FMLA leave.

If an employee was hired for a specific term or only to perform work on a discrete project, the employer has no obligation to restore the employee if the employment term or project is over and the employer would not otherwise have continued to employ the employee. On the other hand, if an employee was hired to perform work on a contract, and after that contract period the contract was awarded to another contractor, the successor contractor may be required to restore the employee if it is a successor employer.

An employer may deny job restoration to key employee (defined elsewhere in this guide) if such denial is necessary to prevent substantial and grievous economic injury to the operations of the employer; or may delay restoration to an employee who fails to provide a fitness-for-duty certificate to return to work under where permitted by the Act.

If the employee is unable to perform an essential function of the position because of a physical or mental condition, including the continuation of a serious health condition or an injury or illness also covered by workers' compensation, the employee has no right to restoration to another position under the FMLA. The employer's obligations may, however, be governed by the Americans with Disabilities Act (ADA), as amended, State leave laws, or workers' compensation laws.

An employee who fraudulently obtains FMLA leave from an employer is not protected by FMLA's job restoration or maintenance of health benefits provisions. If the employer has a uniformly applied policy governing outside or supplemental employment, such a policy may continue to apply to an employee while on FMLA leave. An employer which does not have such a policy may not deny benefits to which an employee is entitled under FMLA on this basis unless the FMLA leave was fraudulently obtained.

Key Employees

A "key employee" is a salaried (as defined by the FLSA) FMLA-eligible employee who is among the highest paid 10 percent of all the employees employed by the employer within 75 miles of the employee's worksite. The determination of the highest paid 10 percent of employee includes consideration of both salaried and non-salaried, eligible and ineligible employees who are employed by the employer within 75 miles of the worksite. Year-to-date earnings are divided by weeks worked by the employee (including weeks in which paid leave was taken). Earnings include wages, premium pay, incen-

tive pay, and nondiscretionary and discretionary bonuses. Earnings do not include incentives whose value
is determined at some future date, such as stock options, certain benefits or other benefits or perquisites.
The determination of whether a salaried employee is
among the highest paid 10 percent is made at the time
the employee gives notice of the need for leave. No more
than 10 percent of the employer's employees within 75
miles of the worksite can be considered key employees.

Denial of Restoration of Key Employee

In order to deny restoration to a key employee, an employer must determine that the restoration of the employee to employment will cause "substantial and grievous economic injury" to the operations of the employer,
not whether the absence of the employee will cause
such substantial and grievous injury. An employer is
permitted to take into account its ability to replace on
a temporary basis (or temporarily do without) the employee on FMLA leave. If permanent replacement is un-
avoidable, the cost of then reinstating the employee can
be considered in evaluating whether substantial and
grievous economic injury will occur from restoration; in
other words, the effect on the operations of the company
of reinstating the employee in an equivalent position.

A precise test cannot be set for the level of hardship or
injury to the employer which must be sustained. If the
reinstatement of a key employee threatens the economic
viability of the firm, that would constitute substantial
and grievous economic injury. A lesser injury which
causes substantial, long term economic injury would
also be sufficient. Minor inconveniences and costs that

the employer would experience in the normal course of doing business would certainly not constitute substantial and grievous economic injury. It is important to note that the FMLA's substantial and grievous economic injury standard is different from and more stringent than the undue hardship test under the Americans With Disabilities Act.

Rights of a Key Employee and Required Notifications

An employer who believes that reinstatement may be denied to a key employee, must give written notice to the employee at the time the employee gives notice of the need for FMLA leave (or when FMLA leave commences, if earlier) that he or she qualifies as a key employee. At the same time, the employer must also fully inform the employee of the potential consequences with respect to reinstatement and maintenance of health benefits if the employer should determine that substantial and grievous economic injury to the employer's operations will result if the employee is reinstated from FMLA leave. If such notice cannot be given immediately because of the need to determine whether the employee is a key employee, it must be given as soon as practicable after being notified of a need for leave (or the commencement of leave, if earlier). It is expected that in most circumstances there will be no desire that an employee be denied restoration after FMLA leave and, therefore, there would be no need to provide such notice. However, an employer who fails to provide such timely notice will lose its right to deny restoration even if substantial and grievous economic injury will result from reinstatement.

As soon as the employer makes a good faith determination, based on the facts available, that substantial and grievous economic injury to its operations will result if a key employee who has given notice of the need for FMLA leave or is using FMLA leave is reinstated, the employer must notify the employee in writing of its determination, that it cannot deny FMLA leave, and that it intends to deny restoration to employment on completion of the FMLA leave. It is anticipated that an employer will ordinarily be able to give such notice prior to the employee starting leave. The employer must serve this notice either in person or by certified mail. This notice must explain the basis for the employer's finding that substantial and grievous economic injury will result, and, if leave has commenced, must provide the employee a reasonable time in which to return to work, taking into account the circumstances, such as the length of the leave and the urgency of the need for the employee to return.

If an employee on leave does not return to work in response to the employer's notification of intent to deny restoration, the employee continues to be entitled to maintenance of health benefits and the employer may not recover its cost of health benefit premiums. A key employee's rights under FMLA continue unless and until the employee either gives notice that he or she no longer wishes to return to work, or the employer actually denies reinstatement at the conclusion of the leave period.

After notice to an employee has been given that substantial and grievous economic injury will result if the employee is reinstated to employment, an employee is still entitled to request reinstatement at the end of the leave period even if the employee did not return to work in response to the employer's notice. The employer must then again determine whether there will be substantial and grievous economic injury from reinstatement, based on the facts at that time. If it is determined that substantial and grievous economic injury will result, the employer must notify the employee in writing (in person or by certified mail) of the denial of restoration.

3

Employer and Employee Rights and Obligations

Employer Notice Requirements

The FMLA requires employers to provide a variety of notices to eligible employees under strict guidelines. Failure to follow the notice requirements described below may constitute an interference with, restraint, or denial of the exercise of an employee's FMLA rights. An employer may be liable for compensation and benefits, for other actual monetary losses sustained, and for appropriate equitable or other relief, including employment, reinstatement, promotion, or any other relief tailored to the harm. Many of these notices are available on the Department of Labor's website for use and/ or adaptation by employers.

General Notice

Every employer covered by the FMLA is required to post and keep posted on its premises, in conspicuous places where employees are employed, a notice explaining the FMLA's provisions and providing information concerning the procedures for filing complaints of violations of the FMLA with the Wage and Hour Division of the United States Department of Labor. The notice must be posted prominently where it can be readily seen by employees and applicants for employment. The poster and the text must be large enough to be easily read and contain fully legible text. Electronic posting may be sufficient to meet this posting requirement. An employer that willfully violates the posting requirement may be assessed a civil money penalty by the Wage and Hour Division not to exceed $110 for each separate offense. Covered employers must post this general notice even if no employees are eligible for FMLA leave.

If an FMLA-covered employer has any eligible employees, it is also required to provide this general notice to each employee by including the notice in employee handbooks or other written guidance to employees concerning employee benefits or leave rights, if such written materials exist, or by distributing a copy of the general notice to each new employee upon hiring. In either case, distribution may be accomplished electronically.

An approved document may be obtained from the Department of Labor for this purpose. Employers are, however, permitted to use another format so long as the information provided includes, at a minimum, all of the information contained in that notice. Where an employer's workforce is comprised of a significant portion of workers who are not literate in English, the employer must provide the general notice in a language in which the employees are literate. Prototypes are available from the Department of Labor. Employers furnishing FMLA notices to sensory impaired individuals must also comply with all applicable requirements under Federal or State law.

Eligibility Notice

When an employee requests FMLA leave, or when the employer acquires knowledge that an employee's leave may be for an FMLA-qualifying reason, the employer must notify the employee of the employee's eligibility to take FMLA leave within five business days, absent extenuating circumstances. Employee eligibility is determined (and notice must be provided) at the commencement of the first instance of leave for each FMLA qualifying reason in the applicable 12-month period. All FMLA absences for the same qualifying reason are considered a single leave and employee eligibility as to that reason for leave does not change during the applicable 12-month period.

The eligibility notice must state whether the employee is eligible for FMLA leave as defined. If the employee is not eligible for FMLA leave, the notice must state at least one reason why the employee is not eligible, including, as applicable, the number of months the employee has been employed by the employer, the number of hours of service worked for the employer during the 12-month period, and whether the employee is employed at a worksite where 50 or more employees are employed by the employer within 75 miles of that work-site. Notification of eligibility may be oral or in writing; employers may use an approved form available on the Department of Labor's website for this purpose. Where an employer's workforce is comprised of a significant portion of workers who are not literate in English, the employer must provide the eligibility notice in a language in which the employees are literate.

If, at the time an employee provides notice of a sub-sequent need for FMLA leave during the applicable 12-month period due to a different FMLA-qualifying reason, the employee's eligibility status has not changed, no additional eligibility notice is required. If, however, the employee's eligibility status has changed (i.e. if the employee has worked fewer than 1,250 hours of service for the employer in the 12 months preceding the commencement of leave for the subsequent qualifying reason or the size of the workforce at the worksite has dropped below 50 employees), the employer must notify the employee of the change in eligibility status within five business days, absent extenuating circumstances.

Notice of Rights and Responsibilities

Employers are required to provide written notice detailing the specific expectations and obligations of the employee and explaining any consequences of a failure to meet these obligations. Typically this is in the form of an employer policy. Where an employer's workforce is comprised of a significant portion of workers who are not literate in English, the employer must provide this notice in a language in which the employees are literate. This notice must be provided to the employee each time the eligibility notice is provided (as described above). If leave has already begun, the notice should be mailed to the employee's address of record. This notice of rights and responsibilities may be distributed electronically.

The required elements of this notice include, as appropriate,

1. that the leave may be designated and counted against the employee's annual FMLA leave entitlement if qualifying and the applicable 12-month period for FMLA entitlement,

2. any requirements for the employee to furnish certification of a serious health condition, serious injury or illness, or qualifying exigency arising out of active duty or call to active duty status, and the consequences of failing to do so,

3. the employee's right to substitute paid leave, whether the employer will require the substitution of paid leave, the conditions related to any substitution, and the employee's entitlement to take unpaid FMLA leave if the employee does not meet the conditions for paid leave,

4. any requirement for the employee to make any premium payments to maintain health benefits and the arrangements for making such payments, and the possible consequences of failure to make such payments on a timely basis (the circumstances under which coverage may lapse),

5. the employee's status as a key employee and the potential consequence that restoration may be denied following FMLA leave, explaining the con-

ditions required for such denial,

6. the employee's rights to maintenance of benefits during the FMLA leave and restoration to the same or an equivalent job upon return from FMLA leave, and,

7. the employee's potential liability for payment of health insurance premiums paid by the employer during the employee's unpaid FMLA leave if the employee fails to return to work after taking FMLA leave.

The notice of rights and responsibilities may include other information, such as, for example, whether the employer will require periodic reports of the employee's status and intent to return to work, but is not required to do so. The notice may be accompanied by any required certification form.

If the specific information provided by the notice of rights and responsibilities changes, the employer must, within five business days of receipt of the employee's first notice of need for leave subsequent to any change, provide written notice referencing the prior notice and setting forth any of the information in the notice of rights and responsibilities that has changed. For example, if the initial leave period was paid leave and the subsequent leave period would be unpaid leave, the employer may need to give notice of the arrangements for making premium payments.

Employers are also expected to responsively answer questions from employees concerning their rights and responsibilities under the FMLA.

Designation Notice

The employer is responsible in all circumstances for designating leave as FMLA-qualifying and for giving notice of the designation to the employee. When the employer has enough information to determine whether the leave is being taken for a FMLA-qualifying reason (such as, for example, after receiving a certification), the employer must notify the employee whether the leave will be designated and will be counted as FMLA leave within five business days, absent extenuating circumstances. Only one notice of designation is required for each FMLA-qualifying reason per applicable 12-month period, regardless of whether the leave taken due to the qualifying reason will be a continuous block of leave or intermittent or reduced schedule leave. If the employer determines that the leave will not be designated as FMLA-qualifying (i.e. if the leave is not for a reason covered by FMLA or the FMLA leave entitlement has been exhausted), the employer must notify the employee of that determination. If the employer requires paid leave to be substituted for unpaid FMLA leave, or that paid leave taken under an existing leave plan be counted as FMLA leave, the employer must inform the employee of this designation at the time of designating the FMLA leave. If the employer has sufficient information to designate the leave as FMLA leave immediately after receiving notice of the employee's need for leave, the employer may provide the employee with the designation notice at that time.

If the employer will require the employee to present a fitness-for-duty certification to be restored to employment, the employer must provide notice of such requirement with the designation notice. If the employer will require that the fitness-for-duty certification address the employee's ability to perform the essential functions of the employee's position, the employer must so indicate in the designation notice and must include a list of the essential functions of the employee's position. If the employer handbook or other written documents describing the employer's leave policies clearly provide that a fitness-for-duty certification will be required in specific circumstances (i.e. by stating that fitness-for-duty certification will be required in all cases of back injuries for employees in a certain occupation), the employer is not required to provide written notice of the requirement with the designation notice, but must provide oral notice no later than with the designation notice.

The designation notice must be in writing. A sample designation notice is available on the Department of Labor's website for adaptation by the employer. However, if the leave is not designated as FMLA leave because it does not meet the requirements of the Act, the notice to the employee that the leave is not designated as FMLA leave may be in the form of a simple written statement.

If the information provided by the employer to the employee in the designation notice changes (such as would occur, for example, when the employee exhausts all of his/her FMLA leave entitlement), the employer must provide, within five business days of receipt of the employee's first notice of need for leave subsequent to any change, written notice of that change.

The employer must notify the employee of the amount of leave counted against the employee's FMLA leave entitlement. If the amount of leave needed is known at the time the employer designates the leave as FMLA qualifying, the employer must notify the employee of the number of hours, days, or weeks that will be counted against the employee's FMLA leave entitlement in the designation notice. If it is not possible to provide the hours, days, or weeks that will be counted against the employee's FMLA leave entitlement (such as in the case of unforeseeable intermittent leave), then the employer must provide notice of the amount of leave counted against the employee's FMLA leave entitlement upon the request by the employee, but no more often than once in a 30-day period and only if leave was taken in that period. The notice of the amount of leave counted against the employee's FMLA entitlement may be oral or in writing. If such notice is oral, it must be confirmed in writing, no later than the following payday (unless the payday is less than one week after the oral notice, in which case the notice must be no later than the subsequent payday). Such written notice may be in any form, including a notation on the employee's pay stub.

Designation of FMLA Leave

Employer Responsibilities

The employer's decision to designate leave as FMLA-qualifying must be based only on information received from the employee or the employee's spokesperson (such as, for example, the employee's spouse or other representative in the event the employee is incapacitated). In any circumstance where the employer does not have sufficient information about the reason for an employee's use of leave, the employer should inquire further of the employee or the spokesperson to ascertain whether leave is potentially FMLA-qualifying. Once the employer has acquired knowledge that the leave is being taken for a FMLA-qualifying reason, the employer must notify the employee as described in the section on employer notice requirements above.

Employee Responsibilities

An employee giving notice of the need for FMLA leave does not need to expressly assert rights under the FMLA or even mention the FMLA to meet his or her obligation to provide notice, though the employee would need to state a qualifying reason for the needed leave and otherwise satisfy the notice requirements described below in the section on Employee Notice Requirements. Generally, an employee giving notice of the need for FMLA leave must explain the reasons for the needed leave to allow the employer to determine whether the leave qualifies as FMLA leave. If the employee fails to explain the reasons, leave may be denied. In many cases, in explaining the reasons for a request to use leave, especially when the need for the leave was unexpected or unforeseen, an employee will provide sufficient information for the employer to designate the leave as FMLA leave. An employee using accrued paid leave may, in some cases, not spontaneously explain the reasons or their plans for using their accrued leave. However, if an employee requesting to use paid leave for a FMLA-qualifying reason does not explain the reason for the leave and the employer denies the employee's request, the employee will need to provide sufficient information to establish a FMLA-qualifying reason for the needed leave so that the employer is aware that the leave may not be denied and may designate that the paid leave be appropriately counted against (substituted for) the employee's FMLA leave entitlement. Similarly, an employee using accrued paid vacation leave who seeks an extension of unpaid leave for a FMLA-qualifying reason will need to state the reason. If this is due to an event which occurred during the period of paid leave, the employer may count the leave used after the FMLA-qualifying reason against the employee's FMLA leave entitlement. If there is a dispute between an employer and an employee as to whether leave qualifies as FMLA leave, it should be resolved through discussions between the employee and the employer. The FMLA Regulations require that these discussions and the ultimate decision be documented.

If an employer does not designate leave in the normal course, the employer may retroactively designate leave as FMLA leave with appropriate notice to the employee as long as the employer's failure to timely designate leave does not cause harm or injury to the employee. In all cases where leave would qualify for FMLA protections, an employer and an employee can mutually agree that leave be retroactively designated as FMLA leave.

Remedies for the Employee When the Employer Fails to Timely Designate Leave

If an employer fails to timely designate leave appropriately and that failure causes harm to the employee, it may constitute an interference with, restraint of, or denial of the exercise of an employee's FMLA rights. Accordingly, the employer may be liable for compensation and benefits lost, for other actual monetary losses sustained, and for appropriate equitable or other relief, including employment, reinstatement, promotion, or any other relief tailored to the harm suffered. The regulations provide the following example to illustrate this point: if an employer that was put on notice that an employee needed FMLA leave failed to designate the leave properly, but the employee's own serious health condition prevented him or her from returning to work during that time period regardless of the designation, an employee may not be able to show that the employee suffered harm as a result of the employer's actions. However, if an employee took leave to provide care for a son or daughter with a serious health condition believing it would not count toward his or her FMLA entitlement, and the employee planned to later use that FMLA leave to provide care for a spouse who would need assistance when recovering from surgery planned for a later date, the employee may be able to show that harm has occurred as a result of the employer's failure to designate properly. The employee might establish this by showing that he or she would have arranged for an alternative caregiver for the seriously ill son or daughter if the leave had been designated timely.

Employee Notice Requirements

Employee Notice Requirements for Foreseeable FMLA Leave

An employee must provide the employer at least 30-days advance notice before FMLA leave is to begin if the need for the leave is foreseeable based on an expected birth, placement for adoption or foster care, planned medical treatment for a serious health condition of the employee or of a family member, or the planned medical treatment for a serious injury or illness of a covered servicemember. If 30 days notice is not practicable (such as because of a lack of knowledge of approximately when leave will be required to begin, a change in circumstances, or a medical emergency), notice must be given as soon as practicable. For example, an employee's health condition may require leave to commence earlier than anticipated before the birth of a child. Similarly, little opportunity for notice may be given before placement for adoption. For foreseeable leave due to a qualifying exigency, notice must be provided as soon as practicable, regardless of how far in advance the leave is foreseeable. Whether FMLA leave is to be continuous or is to be taken intermittently or on a reduced schedule basis, notice need only be given one time, but the employee must advise the employer as soon as practicable if dates of scheduled leave change or are extended, or were initially unknown. In those cases where the employee is required to provide at least 30 days notice of foreseeable leave and does not do so, the employee must explain the reasons why such notice was not practicable upon a request from the employer for such information.

As soon as practicable means as soon as both possible and practical, taking into account all of the facts and circumstances in the individual case. When an employee becomes aware of a need for FMLA leave less than 30 days in advance, it should be practicable for the employee to provide notice of the need for leave either the same day or the next business day. In all cases, however, the determination of when an employee could practicably provide notice must take into account the individual facts and circumstances.

An employee must provide at least verbal notice with sufficient information to make the employer aware that the employee needs FMLA leave, and the anticipated timing and duration of the leave. Depending on the situation, this information may include that a condition renders the employee unable to perform the functions of the job; that the employee is pregnant or has been hospitalized overnight; whether the employee or the employee's family member is under the continuing care of a health care provider; if the leave is due to a qualifying exigency, that a covered military member is on active duty or call to active duty status, and that the requested leave can be classified as a qualifying exigency; if the leave is for a family member, that the condition renders the family member unable to perform daily activities, or that the family member is a covered servicemember with a serious injury or illness; and the anticipated duration of the absence, if known.

When an employee seeks leave for the first time for a FMLA-qualifying reason, the employee need not expressly assert rights under the FMLA or even mention the FMLA. When an employee seeks leave due to a FMLA-qualifying reason, for which the employer has previously provided FMLA-protected leave, the employee must specifically reference the qualifying reason for leave or the need for FMLA leave. In all cases, however, the employer should inquire further of the employee if it is necessary to have more information about whether FMLA leave is being sought by the employee, and obtain the necessary details of the leave to be taken. In the case of medical conditions, the employer may find it necessary to inquire further to determine if the leave is because of a serious health condition and may request medical certification to support the need for such leave. An employer may also request certification to support the need for leave for a qualifying exigency or for military caregiver leave. When an employee has been previously certified for leave due to more than one FMLA-qualifying reason, the employer may need to inquire further to determine for which qualifying reason the leave is needed. An employee has an obligation to respond to an employer's questions designed to determine whether an absence is potentially FMLA-qualifying. Failure to respond to reasonable employer inquiries regarding the leave request may result in denial of FMLA protection if the employer is unable to determine whether the leave is FMLA qualifying.

An employer may certainly require an employee to comply with its standard notice and procedural requirements for requesting leave, absent unusual circumstances. For example, an employer may require that written notice set forth the reasons for the requested leave, the anticipated duration of the leave, and the anticipated start of the leave. An employee also may be required by an employer's policy to contact a specific individual. Unusual circumstances would include situations such as when an employee is unable to comply with the employer's policy that requests for leave should be made by contacting a specific number because on the day the employee needs to provide notice of his or her need for FMLA leave there is no one to answer the call-in number and the voice mail box is full. Where an employee does not comply with the employer's usual notice and procedural requirements, and no unusual circumstances justify the failure to comply, FMLA-protected leave may be delayed or denied. However, FM-

LA-protected leave may not be delayed or denied where the employer's policy requires notice to be given sooner than the notice requirements described above.

When planning medical treatment, the employee is required to consult with the employer and make a reasonable effort to schedule the treatment so as not to disrupt unduly the employer's operations, subject to the approval of the health care provider. Employees are ordinarily expected to consult with their employers prior to the scheduling of treatment in order to work out a treatment schedule which best suits the needs of both the employer and the employee. For example, if an employee who provides notice of the need to take FMLA leave on an intermittent basis for planned medical treatment neglects to consult with the employer to make a reasonable effort to arrange the schedule of treatments so as not to unduly disrupt the employer's operations, the employer may initiate discussions with the employee and require the employee to attempt to make such arrangements, subject to the approval of the health care provider.

Intermittent leave or leave on a reduced schedule leave must be medically necessary due to a serious health condition or a serious injury or illness. An employee must advise the employer, upon request, of the reasons why the intermittent/reduced schedule leave is necessary and of the schedule for treatment, if applicable. The employee and employer are required to attempt to work out a schedule for the leave that meets the employee's needs without unduly disrupting the employer's operations, subject to the approval of the health care provider.

126

Employee Notice Requirements for Unforeseeable FMLA Leave

When the timing of the need for leave is not foreseeable, an employee must provide notice to the employer as soon as practicable under the facts and circumstances of the particular case. It generally should be practicable for the employee to provide notice of leave that is unforeseeable within the time prescribed by the employer's usual and customary notice requirements applicable to such leave. Notice may be given by the employee's spokesperson (such as a spouse, adult family member, or other responsible party) if the employee is unable to do so personally. For example, if an employee's child has a severe asthma attack and the employee takes the child to the emergency room, the employee would not be required to leave his or her child in order to report the absence while the child is receiving emergency treatment. However, if the child's asthma attack required only the use of an inhaler at home followed by a period of rest, the employee would be expected to call the employer promptly after ensuring the child has successfully used the inhaler.

An employee must provide sufficient information for an employer to reasonably determine whether the FMLA may apply to the leave request. Depending on the situation, such information may include that a condition renders the employee unable to perform the functions of the job; that the employee is pregnant or has been hospitalized overnight; whether the employee or the employee's family member is under the continuing care of a health care provider; if the leave is due to a qualifying exigency, that a covered military member is on active duty or call to active duty status, that the requested

127

leave can be considered a qualifying exigency leave, and the anticipated duration of the absence; or if the leave is for a family member that the condition renders the family member unable to perform daily activities or that the family member is a covered servicemember with a serious injury or illness; and the anticipated duration of the absence, if known.

When an employee seeks leave for the first time for a FMLA-qualifying reason, the employee need not expressly assert rights under the FMLA or even mention the FMLA. When an employee seeks leave due to a qualifying reason, for which the employer has previously provided the employee FMLA-protected leave, the employee must specifically reference either the qualifying reason for leave or the need for FMLA leave. Calling in "sick" without providing more information will not be considered sufficient notice to trigger an employer's obligations under the Act. The employer will be expected to obtain any additional required information through informal means. An employee has an obligation to respond to an employer's questions designed to determine whether an absence is potentially FMLA qualifying. Failure to respond to reasonable employer inquiries regarding the leave request may result in denial of FMLA protection if the employer is unable to determine whether the leave is FMLA qualifying.

When the need for leave is not foreseeable, an employee must still comply with the employer's usual and customary notice and procedural requirements for requesting leave, absent unusual circumstances. For example, an employer may require employees to call a designated number or a specific individual to request leave. However, if an employee requires emergency medical treatment, he or she would not be required to follow the call-in procedure until his or her condition is stabilized and he or she has access to, and is able to use, a phone. Similarly, in the case of an emergency requiring leave because of a FMLA-qualifying reason, written advance notice pursuant to an employer's internal rules and procedures may not be required when FMLA leave is involved. If an employee does not comply with the employer's usual notice and procedural requirements, and no unusual circumstances justify the failure to comply, FMLA-protected leave may be delayed or denied.

Employee Failure to Provide Notice

Whenever the commencement of an employee's FMLA leave is to be delayed due to lack of required notice, it must be clear that the employee had actual notice of the FMLA notice requirements. This condition would be satisfied by the employer's proper posting of the required notice at the worksite where the employee is employed and the employer's proper distribution of the notice.

When the need for FMLA leave is foreseeable at least 30 days in advance and an employee fails to give timely advance notice with no reasonable excuse, the employer may delay FMLA coverage until 30 days after the date the employee provides notice. The need for leave and the approximate date leave would be taken must have been clearly foreseeable to the employee 30 days in advance of the leave. For example, knowledge that an employee would receive a telephone call about the availability of a child for adoption at some unknown point in the future would not be sufficient to establish the leave was clearly foreseeable 30 days in advance.

When the need for FMLA leave is foreseeable fewer than 30 days in advance and an employee fails to give notice as soon as practicable under the particular facts and circumstances, the extent to which an employer may delay FMLA coverage for leave depends on the facts of the particular case. For example, if an employee reasonably should have given the employer two weeks' notice but instead only provided one week notice, then the employer may delay FMLA-protected leave for one week.

When the need for FMLA leave is unforeseeable and an employee fails to give proper notice, the extent to which an employer may delay FMLA coverage for leave depends on the facts of the particular case. For example, if it would have been practicable for an employee to have given the employer notice of the need for leave very soon after the need arises consistent with the employer's policy, but instead the employee provided notice two days after the leave began, then the employer may delay FMLA coverage of the leave by two days.

An employer may always waive its employees' FMLA notice obligations or its own internal rules on leave notice requirements. If an employer does not waive the employee's obligations under its internal leave rules, the employer may take appropriate action under its internal rules and procedures for failure to follow its usual and customary notification rules, absent unusual circumstances, as long as the actions are taken in a manner that does not discriminate against employees taking FMLA leave.

Certification

Generally Required Elements

An employer may require that an employee's leave to care for the employee's covered family member with a serious health condition, or due to the employee's own serious health condition that makes the employee unable to perform one or more of the essential functions of the employee's position, be supported by a certification issued by the health care provider of the employee or the employee's family member. An employer may also require that an employee's leave because of a qualifying exigency or to care for a covered servicemember with a serious injury or illness be supported by appropriate certification. An employer is required to give notice of a requirement for certification each time a certification is required; the notice must be in writing whenever required. An employer's oral request to an employee to furnish any subsequent certification is sufficient.

The employer should generally request that an employee furnish certification at the time the employee gives notice of the need for leave or within five business days thereafter, or, in the case of unforeseen leave, within five business days after the leave commences. The employer may request certification at some later date if the employer later has reason to question the appropriateness of the leave or its duration. The employee must provide the requested certification to the employer within 15 calendar days after the employer's request, unless it is not practicable under the particular circumstances to do so despite the employee's diligent, good faith efforts or if the employer provides more than 15 calendar days to return the requested certification.

The certification provided by the employee must be complete and sufficient if so required by the employer. The employer must advise the employee whenever it determines that the provided certification is incomplete or insufficient. In such an instance, the employer is required to document, in writing, what additional information is necessary to make the certification complete and sufficient. A certification is considered incomplete if the employer receives a certification but one or more of the applicable entries have not been completed or if on a completed certification the information provided is vague, ambiguous, or non-responsive. The employer must provide the employee with seven calendar days (unless not practicable under the particular circumstances despite the employee's diligent good faith efforts) to cure any such deficiency. If the deficiencies specified by the employer are not cured in the resubmitted certification, the employer may deny the taking of FMLA leave. A certification that is not returned to the employer is not considered incomplete or insufficient but constitutes a failure to provide certification.

At the time the employer requests certification, it must also advise an employee of the anticipated consequences of his/her failure to provide adequate certification. If the employee fails to provide the employer with a complete and sufficient certification, despite the opportunity to cure the certification, or fails to provide any certification, the employer may deny FMLA leave. It is the employee's responsibility either to furnish a complete and sufficient certification or to furnish the health care provider providing the certification with any necessary authorization from the employee or the employee's family member in order for the health care provider to release a complete and sufficient certification to the employer to support the employee's FMLA request. This rule applies in the instances of whether it is the initial certification, a recertification, a second or third opinion, or a fitness-for-duty certificate, including any clarifications necessary to determine if the certifications are authentic and sufficient.

Where the employee's need for leave due to the employee's own serious health condition or the serious health condition of the employee's covered family member, lasts beyond a single leave year, the employer may require the employee to provide a new medical certification in each subsequent leave year.

Content of the Medical Certification - Employee's Own Serious Health Condition or that of a Family Member

When FMLA leave is taken because of an employee's own serious health condition or the serious health condition of a family member, an employer may require an employee to obtain a medical certification from a health care provider that sets forth the following information:

1. The name, address, telephone number, and fax number of the health care provider and type of medical practice/specialization;

2. The approximate date on which the serious health condition commenced, and its probable duration;

3. A statement or description of appropriate medical facts regarding the patient's health condition for which FMLA leave is requested supporting

need for leave. These may include information concerning symptoms, diagnosis, hospitalization, doctor visits, whether medication has been prescribed, any referrals for evaluation or treatment or any other regimen of continuing treatment;

4. If the employee is the patient, information sufficient to establish that the employee cannot perform the essential functions of the employee's job as well as the nature of any other work restrictions, and the likely duration of such inability;

5. If the patient is a covered family member with a serious health condition, information sufficient to establish that the family member is in need of care, and an estimate of the frequency and duration of the leave required to care for the family member;

6. If an employee requests leave on an intermittent or reduced schedule basis for planned medical treatment of the employee's or a covered family member's serious health condition, information sufficient to establish the medical necessity for the intermittent or reduced schedule leave and an estimate of the dates and duration of such treatments and any periods of recovery;

7. If an employee requests leave on an intermittent or reduced schedule basis for the employee's serious health condition, including pregnancy, that may result in unforeseeable episodes of incapacity, information sufficient to establish the medical necessity for the intermittent or reduced schedule leave and an estimate of the frequency and duration of the episodes of incapacity; and

8. If an employee requests leave on an intermittent or reduced schedule basis to care for a covered family member with a serious health condition, a statement that such leave is medically necessary to care for the family member, which can include assisting in the family member's recovery, and an estimate of the frequency and duration of the required leave.

The United States Department of Labor has developed two optional forms (Form WH–380E and Form WH–380F, as revised) for use in obtaining medical certification, including second and third opinions, from health care providers that meet the FMLA's certification requirements. In addition, Form WH–380E can be used when the employee's need for leave is due to the employee's own serious health condition. Form WH–380F is for use when the employee needs leave to care for a family member with a serious health condition. These optional forms reflect certification requirements to permit the health care provider to furnish appropriate medical information. Forms WH–380E and WH–380F, as revised, or another form containing the same basic information, may be used by the employer; however, no information may be required beyond that permitted by the FMLA. In all instances the information on the form must relate only to the serious health condition for which the current need for leave exists.

If an employee is on FMLA leave running concurrently with a workers' compensation absence, and the provisions of the workers' compensation statute permit the employer or the employer's representative to request additional information from the employee's workers' compensation health care provider, the FMLA does not prevent the employer from following the workers' compensation provisions, and information received under those provisions may be considered in determining the employee's entitlement to FMLA-protected leave. Similarly, an employer may request additional information in accordance with a paid leave policy or disability plan that requires greater information to qualify for payments or benefits, provided that the employer informs the employee that the additional information only needs to be provided in connection with receipt of such payments or benefits. Any information received pursuant to such policy or plan may be considered in determining the employee's entitlement to FMLA-protected leave. If the employee fails to provide the information required for receipt of such payments or benefits, such failure will not affect the employee's entitlement to take unpaid FMLA leave.

If an employee's serious health condition may also be a disability under the Americans with Disabilities Act (ADA), as amended, the FMLA does not prevent the employer from following the procedures for requesting medical information under the ADA. Any information received pursuant to these procedures may be considered in determining the employee's entitlement to FMLA-protected leave.

While an employee may choose to comply with the certification requirement by providing the employer with an authorization, release, or waiver allowing the employer to communicate directly with the health care provider of the employee or his or her covered family member, the employee may not be required to provide such an authorization, release, or waiver. In all instances in which certification is requested, it is the employee's responsibility to provide the employer with complete and sufficient certification, and failure to do so may result in the denial of FMLA leave.

Authentication and Clarification of Medical Certification - Employee's own Serious Health Condition or that a Family Member; Second and Third Opinions

If an employee submits a complete and sufficient certification signed by the health care provider, the employer may not request additional information from the health care provider. However, the employer may contact the health care provider for purposes of clarification and authentication of the medical certification (whether initial certification or recertification) after the employer has given the employee an opportunity to cure any deficiencies in the certification. To make contact with the health care provider, the employer must use a health care provider, a human resources professional, a leave administrator, or a management official. Under no circumstances, however, may the employee's direct supervisor contact the employee's health care provider.

"Authentication'" means providing the health care provider with a copy of the certification and requesting verification that the information contained on the certification form was completed and/or authorized by the health care provider who signed the document; no additional medical information may be requested. "Clarification" means contacting the health care provider to understand the handwriting on the medical certification or to understand the meaning of a response. Employers may not ask health care providers for additional information beyond that required by the certification form. The requirements of the Health Insurance Portability and Accountability Act ("HIPAA") Privacy Rule which governs the privacy of individually-identifiable health information created or held by HIPAA covered entities, must be satisfied when individually-identifiable health information of an employee is shared with an employer by a HIPAA-covered health care provider. If an employee chooses not to provide the employer with authorization allowing the employer to clarify the certification with the health care provider, and does not otherwise clarify the certification, the employer may deny the taking of FMLA leave if the certification is unclear. It is the employee's responsibility to provide the employer with a complete and sufficient certification and to clarify the certification if necessary.

When an employer has reason to doubt the validity of a medical certification, it may require the employee to obtain a second opinion at the employer's expense. Pending receipt of the second (or third) medical opinion, the employee is provisionally entitled to FMLA benefits, including maintenance of group health benefits. If the certifications do not ultimately establish the employee's entitlement to FMLA leave, the leave will not be designated as FMLA leave and may be treated as paid or unpaid leave under the employer's established leave policies, if such leaves of absence exist. The employer is permitted to designate the health care provider to furnish the second opinion, but the selected health care provider may not be employed on a regular basis by the employer. The employer may not regularly contract with or otherwise regularly utilize the services of the health care provider furnishing the second opinion unless the employer is located in an area where access to health care is extremely limited (such as a rural area where no more than one or two doctors practice in the relevant specialty in the vicinity).

If the opinions of both the employee's and the employer's designated health care providers differ, the employer may require the employee to obtain certification from a third health care provider, again at the employer's expense. This third opinion will be final and binding. The third health care provider must be designated or approved jointly by the employer and the employee. The employer and the employee must each act in good faith to attempt to reach agreement on the provider selected for the third opinion. If the employer does not attempt in good faith to reach agreement, the employer will be bound by the first certification. If the employee does not attempt in good faith to reach agreement, the employee will be bound by the second certification. For example, an employee who refuses to agree to see a doctor in the specialty in question may be failing to act in good faith. On the other hand, an employer that refuses to agree to any doctor on a list of specialists in the appropriate field provided by the employee and whom the employee has not previously consulted may be failing to act in good faith.

The employer is required to provide the employee with a copy of the second and third medical opinions, where applicable, upon request by the employee. These copies must be provided within five business days unless extenuating circumstances prevent such action. If the employer requires the employee to obtain either a second or third opinion, the employer must reimburse an employee or family member for any reasonable out of pocket travel expenses incurred to obtain the second and third medical opinions. The employer may not require the employee or family member to travel outside normal commuting distance for purposes of obtaining the second or third medical opinions except in very unusual circumstances.

In the circumstances in which the employee or a family member is visiting in another country, or a family member resides in another country, and a serious health condition develops, the employer must accept a medical certification as well as second and third opinions from a health care provider who practices in that country. Where a certification by a foreign health care provider is in a language other than English, the employee must provide the employer with a written translation of the certification upon request.

Recertification – Employee's Own Serious Health Condition or that of a Family Member

An employer may request recertification no more often than every 30 days and only in connection with an absence by the employee, unless one of the following apply:

1. For leaves 30 days or longer: If the medical certification indicates that the minimum duration of the condition is more than 30 days, an employer must wait until that minimum duration expires before requesting a recertification, unless a) the

employee requests an extension of the leave, b) circumstances described by the previous certification have changed significantly (such as the duration or frequency of the absence, the nature or severity of the illness, complications), or c) the employer receives information that casts doubt upon the employee's stated reason for the absence or the continuing validity of the certification. In all cases, an employer may request a recertification of a medical condition every six months. Thus, even if the certification indicates that the employee will need intermittent or reduced schedule leave for a period of more than six months, the employer would be permitted to request recertification every six months for that absence.

2. For leaves of less than 30 days: The employer may ask for recertification if, a) the employee requests an extension of leave or circumstances described by the previous certification have changed significantly (such as the duration or frequency of the absence, the nature or severity of the illness, or complications), or, b) the employer receives information that casts doubt upon the employee's stated reason for the absence or the continuing validity of the certification.

The employee is required to provide the requested recertification to the employer within the timeframe requested by the employer (which must allow at least 15 calendar days after the employer's request), unless it is not practicable under the particular circumstances to do so despite the employee's diligent, good faith efforts.

The employer may ask for the same information when obtaining recertification as that permitted for the original certification. The employee has the same obligations to participate and cooperate (including providing a complete and sufficient certification or adequate authorization to the health care provider) in the recertification process as in the initial certification process. As part of the information allowed to be obtained on recertification for leave taken because of a serious health condition, the employer may provide the health care provider with a record of the employee's absence pattern and ask the health care provider if the serious health condition and need for leave is consistent with such a pattern. The employer is required to bear the cost associated with any recertification requested and may not request recertification on a second or third opinion.

Certification for Leave - Qualifying Exigency

The first time an employee requests leave because of a qualifying exigency arising out of the active duty or call to active duty status of a covered military member, an employer may require the employee to provide a copy of the covered military member's active duty orders or other appropriate documentation showing that the covered military member is on active duty or called to active duty status in support of a contingency operation and the dates of the covered military member's active duty service. The individual needs to only provide this information to the employer once.

A copy of new active duty orders or other documentation issued by the military must be provided if the need for leave because of a qualifying exigency arises out of a different active duty or call to active duty status of the same or a different covered military member.

A certification of leave for any qualifying exigency must include the following information: a) a statement or description, signed by the employee, of appropriate facts regarding the qualifying exigency for which FMLA leave is requested, sufficiently supporting the need for leave (including the type of qualifying exigency and any available written documentation which supports the request for leave), b) the approximate date on which the qualifying exigency commenced or will commence, c) if an employee requests leave because of a qualifying exigency for a single, continuous period of time, the beginning and end dates of the leave, d) if an employee requests leave because of a qualifying exigency on an intermittent or reduced schedule basis, an estimate of the frequency and duration of the qualifying exigency, and e) if the qualifying exigency involves meeting with a third party, appropriate contact information for the individual or entity with whom the employee is meeting (such as the name, title, organization, address, telephone number, fax number, and e-mail address) and a brief description of the purpose of the meeting.

The United States Department of Labor has developed an optional form (Form WH–384) for employees' use in obtaining a certification that meets FMLA's certification requirements. This optional form reflects certification requirements so as to permit the employee to furnish appropriate information to support his or her request for leave because of a qualifying exigency. While use of this form is not required, no information may be required beyond that described above.

If an employee submits a complete and sufficient certification to support his or her request for leave because of a qualifying exigency, the employer may not request additional information from the employee. However, if the qualifying exigency involves meeting with a third party, the employer may contact the individual or entity with whom the employee is meeting for purposes of verifying a meeting or appointment schedule and the nature of the meeting between the employee and the specified individual or entity. The employee's permission is not required in order to verify meetings or appointments with third parties, but no additional information may be requested by the employer. An employer also may contact an appropriate unit of the Department of Defense to request verification that a covered military member is on active duty or call to active duty status; no additional information may be requested and the employee's permission is not required.

Certification for Leave - Covered Servicemember Military Caregiver Leave

When leave is taken to care for a covered servicemember with a serious injury or illness, an employer may require an employee to obtain a certification completed by an authorized health care provider of the covered servicemember. For purposes of leave taken to care for a covered servicemember, any one of the following health care providers may complete such a certification, a) a United States Department of Defense ("DOD") health care provider, b) a United States Department of Veterans Affairs ("VA") health care provider, c) a DOD TRICARE network authorized private health care provider, or d) a DOD non-network TRICARE authorized private health care provider. If the authorized health care provider is unable to make certain military-related determinations as required, he or she may rely on determinations from an authorized DOD representative (such as a DOD recovery care coordinator).

An employer may request that the health care provider provide the following information which largely concern the servicemember:

1. The name, address, and appropriate contact information (telephone number, fax number, and/or e-mail address) of the health care provider, the type of medical practice, the medical specialty, and whether the health care provider is, a) a DOD health care provider, b) a VA health care provider, c) a DOD TRICARE network authorized private health care provider, or d) a DOD non-network TRICARE authorized private health care provider;

2. Whether the covered servicemember's injury or illness was incurred in the line of duty on active duty;

3. The approximate date on which the serious injury or illness commenced, and its probable duration;

4. A statement or description of appropriate medical facts regarding the covered servicemember's health condition for which FMLA leave is requested. The medical facts must be sufficient to support the need for leave, including, for example, information on whether the injury or illness may render the covered servicemember medically unfit to perform the duties of the servicemember's office, grade, rank, or rating and whether

the member is receiving medical treatment, recuperation, or therapy;

5. Information sufficient to establish that the covered servicemember is in need of care and whether the covered servicemember will need care for a single continuous period of time, including any time for treatment and recovery, and an estimate as to the beginning and ending dates for this period of time;

6. If an employee requests leave on an intermittent or reduced schedule basis for planned medical treatment appointments for the covered servicemember, whether there is a medical necessity for the covered servicemember to have such periodic care and an estimate of the treatment schedule of such appointments;

7. If an employee requests leave on an intermittent or reduced schedule basis to care for a covered servicemember other than for planned medical treatment (such as episodic flare-ups of a medical condition), whether there is a medical necessity for the covered servicemember to have such periodic care, which can include assisting in the covered servicemember's recovery, and an estimate of the frequency and duration of the periodic care.

In addition to the information that may be requested regarding the servicemember, the employer may require the certification of additional information which includes:

1. The name and address of the employer of the employee requesting leave to care for a covered ser-

vicemember, the name of the employee requesting such leave, and the name of the covered servicemember for whom the employee is requesting leave to care;

2. The relationship of the employee to the covered servicemember for whom the employee is requesting leave to care for;

3. Whether the covered servicemember is a current member of the Armed Forces, the National Guard or Reserves, and the covered servicemember's military branch, rank, and current unit assignment;

4. Whether the covered servicemember is assigned to a military medical facility as an outpatient or to a unit established for the purpose of providing command and control of members of the Armed Forces receiving medical care as outpatients (such as a medical hold or warrior transition unit) and the name of the medical treatment facility or unit;

5. Whether the covered servicemember is on the temporary disability retired list;

6. A description of the care to be provided to the covered servicemember and an estimate of the leave needed to provide the care.

The United States Department of Labor has developed an optional form (WH–385) for use in obtaining certification that meets FMLA's certification requirements. This optional form reflects certification requirements so as to permit the employee to furnish appropriate information to support his or her request for leave to care for a covered servicemember with a serious injury or illness. The use of WH–385 is not required, and another form containing the same basic information may be used by the employer. No additional information, however, may be required beyond that specified above. The information on the certification must relate only to the serious injury or illness for which the current need for leave exists. An employer may seek authentication and/or clarification of the certification, but second and third opinions are not permitted for leave to care for a covered servicemember. Additionally, recertifications are not permitted for leave to care for a covered servicemember. An employer may require an employee to provide confirmation of covered family relationship to the seriously injured or ill servicemember.

An employer requiring an employee to submit a certification for leave to care for a covered servicemember must accept as sufficient certification, in lieu of form WH–385 or an employer's own certification form, "invitational travel orders" ("ITO's") or "invitational travel authorizations" ("ITA's") issued to any family member to join an injured or ill servicemember at his or her bedside. An ITO or ITA is sufficient certification for the duration of time specified in the ITO or ITA. During that time period, an eligible employee may take leave to care for the covered servicemember in a continuous block of time or on an intermittent basis. An eligible employee who provides an ITO or ITA to support his or her request for leave may not be required to provide any additional or separate certification that leave taken on an intermittent basis during the period of time specified in the ITO or ITA is medically necessary. An ITO or ITA is sufficient certification for an employee entitled to take FMLA leave to care for a covered servicemember regardless of whether the employee is named in the order or authorization. If an employee will need leave to care for a covered servicemember beyond the expiration date specified in an ITO or ITA, an employer may request that the employee have one of the authorized health care providers listed above complete Form WH–385 or the employer's own form as requisite certification for the remainder of the employee's necessary leave period.

An employer may seek authentication and clarification of the ITO or ITA, but the employer may not utilize the second or third opinion process or the recertification process previously discussed during the period of time in which leave is supported by an ITO or ITA. An employer may require an employee to provide confirmation of covered family relationship to the seriously injured or ill servicemember when an employee supports his or her request for FMLA leave with a copy of an ITO or ITA. As always, when certification is requested, it is the employee's responsibility to provide the employer with complete and sufficient certification, and failure to do so may result in the denial of FMLA leave.

Intent to Return to Work

An employer may require any employee on FMLA leave to report periodically on his/her status and intent to return to work. The employer's policy regarding such reports may not be discriminatory and must take into account all of the relevant facts and circumstances related to the individual employee's leave situation. If an employee gives unequivocal notice of intent not to return to work, the employer's obligations under FMLA to maintain health benefits (subject to COBRA requirements) and to restore the employee end. However, these obligations continue if an employee indicates he or she may be unable to return to work but expresses a continuing desire to do so.

It may be necessary for an employee to take more leave than originally anticipated. Conversely, an employee may discover after beginning leave that the circumstances have changed and the amount of leave originally anticipated is no longer necessary. An employee may not be required to take more FMLA leave than necessary to resolve the circumstance that precipitated the need for leave. In both of these situations, the employer may require that the employee provide the employer reasonable notice (within two business days) of the changed circumstances where foreseeable. The employer may also obtain information on such changed circumstances through requested status reports.

Fitness-for-Duty Certification

An employer may have a uniformly-applied policy or practice that requires all similarly-situated employees (same occupation or same serious health condition) who take leave for such conditions to obtain and present certification from the employee's health care provider that the employee is able to resume work. The employee has the same obligations to participate and cooperate (including providing a complete and sufficient certification or providing sufficient authorization to the health care provider to provide the information directly to the employer) in the fitness-for-duty certification process as in the initial certification process.

The employer may seek a fitness-for-duty certification only with regard to the particular health condition that caused the employee's need for FMLA leave. The certification from the employee's health care provider must certify that the employee is able to resume work. Additionally, an employer may require that the certification specifically address the employee's ability to perform the essential functions of the employee's job. In order to require such a certification, an employer must provide an employee with a list of the essential functions of the employee's job and must indicate in the designation notice that the certification must address the employee's ability to perform those essential functions. If the employer satisfies these requirements, the employee's health care provider must certify that the employee can perform the identified essential functions of his or her job. Following the procedures previously described, the employer may contact the employee's health care provider for purposes of clarifying and authenticating the fitness-for-duty certification. Clarification may be requested only for the serious health condition for which FMLA leave was taken. The employer may not delay the employee's return to work while contact with the health care provider is being made. No second or third opinions on a fitness-for-duty certification may be required.

The employee is responsible for bearing the cost of this certification and he/she is not entitled to be paid for the time or travel costs spent in acquiring the certification.

At the time that an employer initially designates the employee's leave as FMLA qualifying, the employer is required to advise the employee if it will require a fitness-for-duty certification to return to work and whether that fitness-for-duty certification must address the employee's ability to perform the essential functions of the employee's job. An employer may delay restoration to employment until an employee submits a required fitness-for-duty certification unless the employer has failed to provide the notice of the required fitness-for-duty certification in its initial designation of FMLA leave notice. If an employer provides the notice required, an employee who does not provide a fitness-for-duty certification or request additional FMLA leave is no longer entitled to reinstatement.

An employer is not entitled to a certification of fitness to return to duty for each absence taken on an intermittent or reduced schedule leave. However, an employer is entitled to a certification of fitness to return to duty for such absences up to once every 30 days if reasonable safety concerns exist regarding the employee's ability to perform his or her duties based on the serious health condition for which the employee took such leave. If an employer chooses to require a fitness-for-duty certification under these circumstances, the employer must inform the employee at the same time it issues the designation notice that for each subsequent instance of intermittent or reduced schedule leave; the employee will be required to submit a fitness-for-duty certification unless one has already been submitted within the past 30 days. Alternatively, an employer can set a different interval for requiring a fitness-for-duty certification as long as it does not exceed once every 30 days and as long as the employer advises the employee of the requirement in advance of the employee taking the intermittent or reduced schedule leave. The employer may not terminate the employee while waiting for the certification of fitness to return to duty for an intermittent or reduced schedule leave absence. Reasonable safety concerns means a reasonable belief of significant risk or harm to the individual employee or others. In determining whether reasonable safety concerns exist, an employer should consider the nature and severity of the potential harm and the likelihood that potential harm will occur.

Employers are cautioned that State and local laws or the terms of a collective bargaining agreement may also govern an employee's return to work. In addition, the requirements under the Americans with Disabilities Act (ADA), as amended, apply as well. After an employee returns from FMLA leave, the ADA requires any medical examination, at an employer's expense, by the employer's health care provider be job-related and consistent with business necessity. For example, an employer may require a warehouse laborer, whose back impairment affects the ability to lift, to be examined by an orthopedist, but may not require this employee to submit to an HIV test where the test is not related to either the essential functions of his/her job or to his/her impairment. If an employee's serious health condition may also be a disability within the meaning of the ADA, the FMLA does not prevent the employer from following the procedures for requesting medical information under the ADA.

Failure to Provide Certification

In the case of foreseeable leave, if an employee fails to provide certification in a timely manner as required under the law, an employer may deny FMLA coverage until the required certification is provided. For example, if an employee has 15 days to provide a certification and does not provide the certification for 45 days without sufficient reason for the delay, the employer can deny FMLA protections for the 30-day period following the expiration of the 15-day time period, if the employee takes leave during such period.

In the case of unforeseeable leave, an employer may deny FMLA coverage for the requested leave if the employee fails to provide a certification within 15 calendar days from receipt of the request for certification unless not practicable due to extenuating circumstances. For example, in the case of a medical emergency, it may not be practicable for an employee to provide the required certification within 15 calendar days. Absent such extenuating circumstances, if the employee fails to timely return the certification, the employer can deny FMLA protections for the leave following the expiration of the 15-day time period until a sufficient certification is provided. If the employee never produces the certification, the leave is not FMLA leave.

When requested, an employee must provide recertification of leave within the time requested by the employer (which must allow at least 15 calendar days after the request) or as soon as practicable under the particular facts and circumstances. If an employee fails to provide a recertification within a reasonable time under the particular facts and circumstances, then the employer may deny continuation of the FMLA leave until the employee produces a sufficient recertification. If the employee never produces the recertification, the leave is not FMLA leave. Recertification does not apply to leave taken for a qualifying exigency or to care for a covered servicemember.

When a fitness-for-duty certification is requested by the employer pursuant to a uniformly applied policy for similarly-situated employees, the employee must provide medical certification, at the time the employee seeks reinstatement, at the end of FMLA leave taken for the employee's serious health condition, that the employee is fit for duty and able to return to work if the employer has provided the required notice. The employer may delay restoration until the certification is provided. Unless the employee provides either a fitness-for-duty certification or a new medical certification for a serious health condition at the time FMLA leave is concluded, the employee may be terminated.

4

Record Keeping and Enforcement

Record Keeping Requirements

The FMLA requires that covered employers make, keep, and preserve records pertaining to their obligations under the law. It also restricts the authority of the Department of Labor to require any employer, plan, fund, or program to submit books or records more than once during any 12-month period unless the Department has reasonable cause to believe a violation of FMLA exists or the Department is investigating a complaint.

No particular order or form of records is required. However, employers must keep FMLA records for a minimum of three years and make them available for inspection, copying, and transcription by representatives of the Department of Labor upon request. The records may be maintained and preserved on microfilm or other basic source document of an automated data processing memory provided that adequate projection or viewing equipment is available, that the reproductions are clear and identifiable by date or pay period, and that extensions or transcriptions of the information required can be made available upon request. Records kept in computer form must be made available for transcription or copying.

Covered employers who have eligible employees must maintain the following records:

1. Basic payroll and identifying employee data, including name, address, and occupation; rate or basis of pay and terms of compensation; daily and weekly hours worked per pay period; additions to or deductions from wages; and total compensation paid.

2. The dates FMLA leave is taken by FMLA eligible employees. Leave must be designated in records as FMLA leave; leave so designated may not include leave required under State law or an employer plan which is not also covered by FMLA.

3. If FMLA leave is taken by eligible employees in increments of less than one full day, the hours of the leave.

4. Copies of employee notices of leave furnished to the employer under FMLA, if in writing, and copies of all written notices given to employees as

required. These copies may be maintained in employee personnel files.

5. Any documents (including written and electronic records) describing employee benefits or employer policies and practices regarding the taking of paid and unpaid leaves.

6. Premium payments of employee benefits.

7. Records of any dispute between the employer and an eligible employee regarding designation of leave as FMLA leave, including any written statement from the employer or employee of the reasons for the designation and for the disagreement.

Covered employers with no eligible employees must maintain basic payroll and identifying employee data, including name, address, and occupation; rate or basis of pay and terms of compensation; daily and weekly hours worked per pay period; additions to or deductions from wages; and total compensation.

If FMLA-eligible employees are not subject to FLSA's record keeping regulations for purposes of minimum wage or overtime compliance (in other words, they are exempt from FLSA), an employer need not keep a record of actual hours worked, provided that: a) eligibility for FMLA leave is presumed for any employee who has been employed for at least 12 months; and b) with respect to employees who take FMLA leave intermittently or on a reduced schedule leave, the employer and employee agree on the employee's normal schedule or average hours worked each week and put their agreement terms in writing.

Records and documents relating to certifications, recertifications or medical histories of employees or employees' family members, created for purposes of FMLA, must be maintained as confidential medical records in separate files/records from the usual personnel files; and if the ADA, as amended, is also applicable, these records must be maintained in conformance with ADA confidentiality requirements, except that, a) supervisors and managers may be informed regarding necessary restrictions on the work or duties of an employee and necessary accommodations, b) first aid and safety personnel may be informed (when appropriate) if the employee's physical or medical condition might require emergency treatment; and, c) government officials investigating compliance with FMLA (or other pertinent law) may be provided relevant information upon request.

Federal FMLA Notices and Forms

- Form WH-380E – Certification of Health Care Provider for Employee's Serious Health Condition

- Form WH-380F – Certification of Health Care Provider for Family Member's Serious Health Condition

- Form WH-381 – Notice of Eligibly and Rights and Responsibilities

- Form WH-382 – Designation Notice

- Form WH-384 – Certification of Qualifying Exigency for Military Family Leave

- Form WH-385 – Certification for Serious Injury of Illness of Covered Servicemember – For Military Family Leave

- WH Publication 1420 – Your Rights Under the Family and Medical Leave Act of 1993 (Poster)

Protection for Employees and Others who Assert Rights Under the FMLA

The FMLA prohibits interference with an employee's rights under the law and interference with legal proceedings or inquiries relating to an employee's rights. An employer is prohibited from interfering with, restraining, or denying the exercise of (or attempts to exercise) any rights provided by the FMLA and is prohibited from discharging or in any other way discriminating against any person (whether or not an employee) for opposing or complaining about any unlawful practice under the FMLA.

All persons (whether or not employers) are prohibited from discharging or in any other way discriminating against any person (whether or not an employee) because that person has, a) filed any charge, or has instituted (or caused to be instituted) any proceeding under or related to the FMLA, b) given, or is about to give, any information in connection with an inquiry or proceeding relating to a right under the FMLA, or, c) testified, or is about to testify, in any inquiry or proceeding relating to a right under the FMLA.

Conduct that would be considered violations include interfering with, restraining, or denying the exercise of rights provided by the Act. An employer may be liable for compensation and benefits lost by reason of the violation, for other actual monetary losses sustained as a direct result of the violation, and for appropriate equitable or other relief, including employment, reinstatement, promotion, or any other relief tailored to the harm suffered. Interfering with the exercise of an employee's rights would include, for example, not only refusing to authorize FMLA leave, but discouraging an employee from using such leave. It would also include manipulation by a covered employer to avoid responsibilities under the FMLA. The Regulations provide the following examples to illustrate this point: a) transferring employees from one worksite to another for the purpose of reducing worksites or to keep worksites below the 50-employee threshold for employee eligibility under the FMLA, b) changing the essential functions of the job in order to preclude the taking of leave, or, c) reducing hours available to work in order to avoid employee eligibility.

The FMLA's prohibition against interference also prohibits an employer from discriminating or retaliating against an employee or prospective employee for having exercised or attempting to exercise FMLA rights. For example, if an employee on leave without pay would otherwise be entitled to full benefits (other than health benefits), the same benefits would be required to be provided to an employee on unpaid FMLA leave. By the same token, employers cannot use the taking of FMLA leave as a negative factor in employment actions, such as hiring, promotions or disciplinary actions; nor can FMLA leave be counted under "no fault" attendance policies.

Employees cannot waive, nor may employers induce employees to waive, their prospective rights under FMLA. For example, employees (or their collective bargaining representatives) cannot "trade off" the right to take FMLA leave against some other benefit offered by the employer. This does not prevent the settlement or release of FMLA claims by employees based on past employer conduct without the approval of the Department of Labor or a court. Nor does it prevent an employee's voluntary and uncoerced acceptance (not as a condition of employment) of a "light duty" assignment while recovering from a serious health condition. An employee's acceptance of a "light duty" assignment does not constitute a waiver of the employee's prospective rights, including the right to be restored to the same position the employee held at the time the employee's FMLA leave commenced or to an equivalent position. The employee's right to restoration, however, ceases at the end of the applicable 12-month FMLA leave year.

Individuals, and not merely employees, are protected from retaliation for opposing (i.e., filing a complaint about) any practice which is unlawful under the FMLA. They are similarly protected if they oppose any practice which they reasonably believe to be a violation of the Act or regulations.

Enforcement General Rules

The aggrieved employee may file a complaint with the Secretary of Labor; the employee may also choose to file a private lawsuit. If the employee files a private lawsuit, it must be filed within two years after the last action which the employee contends was in violation of the Act, or three years if the violation was willful.

If an employer is found to have violated the FMLA, an employee may recover wages, employment benefits, or other compensation denied or lost. Where no tangible loss has occurred, such as when FMLA leave was unlawfully denied, the employee can recover any actual monetary loss sustained by the employee as a direct result of the violation, such as the cost of providing care, up to a sum equal to 26 weeks of wages for the employee in a case involving leave to care for a covered servicemember or 12 weeks of wages for the employee in a case involving leave for any other FMLA qualifying reason. In addition, the employee may be entitled to interest. An amount equaling the preceding sums may also be awarded as liquidated damages unless the amount is reduced by a court because the violation was in good faith and the employer had reasonable grounds for believing it had not violated the Act. When appropriate, the employee may also obtain appropriate equitable relief, such as employment, reinstatement and promotion. When the employer is found to be in violation, the employee may recover a reasonable attorney's fee, reasonable expert witness fees, and other costs of the action from the employer in addition to any judgment awarded by the court.

Filing a Complaint with the Federal Government

A complaint may be filed in person, by mail or by telephone, with the Wage and Hour Division, Employment Standards Administration of the United States Department of Labor within a reasonable time of when the employee discovers that his or her FMLA rights have been violated. In no event may a complaint be filed more than two years after the action which is alleged to be a violation of FMLA occurred, or three years in the case of a willful violation.

Violations of the Posting Requirement and Penalties

The Department of Labor may impose a civil money penalty for violations of the posting requirement. An employer may obtain a review of the assessment of penalty from the Wage and Hour Regional Administrator for the region in which the alleged violation(s) occurred. If the employer does not seek such a review or fails to do so in a timely manner, the notice of the penalty constitutes the final ruling of the Secretary of Labor. To obtain review, an employer may file a petition with the Wage and Hour Regional Administrator for the region in which the alleged violations occurred. No particular form of petition for review is required, except that the petition must be in writing, should contain the legal and factual bases for the petition, and must be mailed to the Regional Administrator within 15 days of receipt of the notice of penalty. The employer may request an oral hearing which may be conducted by telephone. The decision of the Regional Administrator constitutes the final order of the Secretary.

The Regional Administrator may seek to recover the unpaid penalty pursuant to the Debt Collection Act (DCA), and, in addition to seeking recovery of the unpaid final order, may seek interest and penalties as provided under the DCA. The final order may also be referred to the Solicitor of Labor for collection. The Secretary may file suit in any court of competent jurisdiction to recover the monies due as a result of the unpaid final order, interest, and penalties.

5

Impact of Other Laws

Interaction with State Laws

Nothing in the FMLA supersedes any provision of State
or local law that provides greater family or medical
leave rights than those provided by the FMLA. The
Department of Labor will not, however, enforce State
family or medical leave laws, and States may not enforce the FMLA. Employees are not required to designate whether the leave they are taking is FMLA leave
or leave under State law, and an employer must comply with the appropriate (applicable) provisions of both.
An employer covered by one law and not the other has
to comply only with the law under which it is covered.
Similarly, an employee eligible under only one law must
receive benefits in accordance with that law.

If leave qualifies for FMLA leave and leave under State law, the leave used counts against the employee's entitlement under both laws. Examples provided by the FMLA Regulations of the interaction between FMLA and State laws include the following:

1. If a State law provides 16 weeks of leave entitlement over two years, an employee needing leave due to his or her own serious health condition would be entitled to take 16 weeks one year under State law and 12 weeks the next year under FMLA. Health benefits maintenance under FMLA would be applicable only to the first 12 weeks of leave entitlement each year. If the employee took 12 weeks the first year, the employee would be entitled to a maximum of 12 weeks the second year under FMLA (not 16 weeks). An employee would not be entitled to 28 weeks in one year.

2. If State law provides half-pay for employees temporarily disabled because of pregnancy for six weeks, the employee would be entitled to an additional six weeks of unpaid FMLA leave (or accrued paid leave).

3. If State law provides six weeks of leave, which may include leave to care for a seriously-ill grandparent or a "spouse equivalent," and leave was used for that purpose, the employee is still entitled to his or her full FMLA leave entitlement, as the leave used was provided for a purpose not covered by FMLA. If FMLA leave is used first for a purpose also provided under State law, and State leave has thereby been exhausted, the employer would not be required to provide additional leave to care for the grandparent or spouse equivalent.

4. If State law prohibits mandatory leave beyond the actual period of pregnancy disability, an instructional employee of an educational agency subject to special FMLA rules may not be required to remain on leave until the end of the academic term, as permitted by FMLA under certain circumstances.

Interaction with Federal and State Anti-Discrimination Laws

Nothing in the FMLA modifies or affects any Federal or State law prohibiting discrimination, such as Title VII of the Civil Rights Act of 1964, as amended by the Pregnancy Discrimination Act. The leave provisions of the FMLA are intended to be wholly distinct from the reasonable accommodation obligations of employers covered under the Americans with Disabilities Act (ADA), as amended. Therefore, with respect to Federal law, an employer must provide leave under whichever statutory provision provides the greater rights to employees. When an employer violates both the FMLA and a discrimination law, an employee may be able to recover under either or both statutes.

If an employee is a qualified individual with a disability within the meaning of the ADA, the employer must make reasonable accommodations barring undue hardship, in accordance with the ADA. At the same time, the employer must afford an employee his or her FMLA rights. ADA's "disability" and the FMLA's "serious health condition" are different concepts and must be analyzed separately. The FMLA entitles eligible employees up to 12 weeks of leave in any 12-month period due to their own serious health condition, whereas the ADA allows an indeterminate amount of leave, barring undue hardship, as a reasonable accommodation. The FMLA requires employers to maintain employees' group health plan coverage during FMLA leave on the same conditions as coverage would have been provided if the employee had been continuously employed during the leave period, whereas the ADA does not require maintenance of health insurance unless other employees receive health insurance during leave under the same circumstances.

A reasonable accommodation under the ADA might be accomplished by providing an individual with a disability with a part-time job with no health benefits, assuming the employer did not ordinarily provide health insurance for part-time employees.

However, the FMLA would permit an employee to work a reduced schedule leave until the equivalent of 12 workweeks of leave were used, with group health benefits maintained during this period. The FMLA permits an employer to temporarily transfer an employee who is taking leave intermittently or on a reduced schedule leave for planned medical treatment to an alternative position, whereas the ADA allows an accommodation of reassignment to an equivalent, vacant position only if the employee cannot perform the essential functions of the employee's present position and an accommodation is not possible in the employee's present position, or an accommodation in the employee's present position would cause an undue hardship. The Regulations provide examples to demonstrate the interaction of these two laws:

1. A qualified individual with a disability who is also an "eligible employee" entitled to FMLA leave requests 10 weeks of medical leave as a reasonable accommodation, which the employer grants because it is not an undue hardship. The employer advises the employee that the 10 weeks of leave is also being designated as FMLA leave and will count towards the employee's FMLA leave entitlement. This designation does not prevent the parties from also treating the leave as a reasonable accommodation and reinstating the employee into the same job, as required by the ADA, rather than an equivalent position under FMLA, if that is the greater right available to the employee. At the same time, the employee would be entitled under FMLA to have the employer maintain group health plan coverage during the leave, as that requirement provides the greater right to the employee.

2. If the same employee needed to work part-time (a reduced schedule leave) after returning to his or her same job, the employee would still be entitled under FMLA to have group health plan coverage maintained for the remainder of the two-week equivalent of FMLA leave entitlement, notwithstanding an employer policy that part-time employees do not receive health insurance. This employee would be entitled under the ADA to reasonable accommodations to enable the employee to perform the essential functions of the part-time position. In addition, because the employee is working a part-time schedule as a reasonable accommodation, the FMLA's provision for temporary assignment to a different alternative

position would not apply. Once the employee has exhausted his or her remaining FMLA leave entitlement while working the reduced (part-time) schedule, if the employee is a qualified individual with a disability, and if the employee is unable to return to the same full-time position at that time, the employee might continue to work part time as a reasonable accommodation, barring undue hardship; the employee would then be entitled to only those employment benefits ordinarily provided by the employer to part-time employees.

3. At the end of the FMLA leave entitlement, an employer is required under the FMLA to reinstate the employee in the same or an equivalent position, with equivalent pay and benefits, to that which the employee held when leave commenced. The employer's FMLA obligations would be satisfied if the employer offered the employee an equivalent full-time position. If the employee were unable to perform the essential functions of that equivalent position even with reasonable accommodation, because of a disability, the ADA may require the employer to make a reasonable accommodation at that time by allowing the employee to work part-time or by reassigning the employee to a vacant position, barring undue hardship.

If FMLA entitles an employee to leave, an employer may not, in lieu of FMLA leave entitlement, require an employee to take a job with a reasonable accommodation. However, the ADA may require that an employer offer an employee the opportunity to take such a position. An employer may not change the essential functions of the job in order to deny FMLA leave.

An employee may be on a workers' compensation absence due to an on-the-job injury or illness which also qualifies as a serious health condition under FMLA. The workers' compensation absence and FMLA leave may run concurrently (subject to proper notice and designation by the employer). At some point the health care provider providing medical care pursuant to the workers' compensation injury may certify the employee is able to return to work in a "light duty" position. If the employer offers such a position, the employee is permitted, but not required, to accept the position. As a result, the employee may no longer qualify for payments from the workers' compensation benefit plan, but the employee is entitled to continue on unpaid FMLA leave either until the employee is able to return to the same or equivalent job the employee left or until the 12-week FMLA leave entitlement is exhausted. If the employee returning from the workers' compensation injury is a qualified individual with a disability, he or she will have rights under the ADA.

If an employer requires certifications of an employee's fitness for duty to return to work, as permitted by FMLA under a uniform policy, it must comply with the ADA requirement that a fitness-for-duty physical be job-related and consistent with business necessity.

Under Title VII of the Civil Rights Act of 1964, as amended by the Pregnancy Discrimination Act, an employer should provide the same benefits for women who are pregnant as the employer provides to other employees with short-term disabilities. Because Title VII does not require employees to be employed for a certain period of time to be protected, an employee employed for less than 12 months by the employer (and, therefore, not an "eligible" employee under FMLA) may not be denied maternity leave if the employer normally provides short-term disability benefits to employees with the same tenure who are experiencing other short-term disabilities.

Under the Uniformed Services Employment and Reemployment Rights Act of 1994 (USERRA), veterans are entitled to receive all rights and benefits of employment that they would have obtained if they had been continuously employed. Therefore, under USERRA, a returning servicemember would be eligible for FMLA leave if the months and hours that he or she would have worked for the civilian employer during the period of military service, combined with the months employed and the hours actually worked meet the FMLA eligibility threshold of 12 months and 1,250 hours of employment.

6

Summary of State
Family Leave Laws

Alaska

Alaska provides family leave beyond that of the FMLA,
but the additional state provisions only apply to State
employees and employees of State subdivisions. Employees are eligible for the additional leave if they have
worked at least 35 hours per week for at least 6 consecutive months or 17.5 hours per week for 12 consecutive
months immediately preceding the leave.

An employer must make available to employees whose
health is affected by pregnancy, childbirth or a related
medical condition the same employment benefits and

privileges that it makes available to other temporarily disabled employees. Employees are eligible for 18 weeks of family leave because of pregnancy, childbirth, or adoption within a 12-month period which expires one year after the birth or placement of the child with the employee. Unlike the FMLA, this additional family leave provided to Alaska State employees does not include leave for a child placed with the employee for foster care. Employees are also eligible for 18 weeks of family leave within a 24-month period because of a serious illness of the employee, the employee's spouse, parent, or child. For the purposes of leave to care for the serious illness of the employee's child, child means birth, adoption, foster, stepchild, or legal ward.

The provisions of the Alaska statute do not apply to small facilities where the number of employees within 50 miles is less than 21 during 20 consecutive weeks.

Arizona

Arizona's family and medical leave law only applies to Arizona State employees, not private-sector employees in the state.

Parental leave, leave taken by an employee due to pregnancy, childbirth, miscarriage, abortion, or adoption, may not exceed 12 weeks. An employee does not have to, but may choose to, use accrued paid time off or compensatory time for part of the leave; however, sick leave may only be taken during periods of disability. If an employee chooses not use accrued paid time off, the leave will be without pay. If the leave qualifies as FMLA leave, it will be counted as FMLA leave. Upon returning from the leave, the employee will be returned to his/her position before the leave.

Family leave for either the employee or a family member's serious illness cannot exceed 12 weeks. The employee will be required to use all accrued sick and then annual leave first, and any remaining leave will be unpaid. If the leave qualifies as FMLA leave then the provisions of the FMLA, not Arizona's provisions will govern the employee's return to work.

Arizona also provides State employees with unpaid medical leave that may not exceed 180 days. Medical leave without pay only applies if the employee is unable to work due to a non-job related, seriously incapacitating illness or injury. Prior to being placed on medical leave without pay, the employee must exhaust all paid leave time, including donated time.

California

California has enacted several laws regarding family and medical leave. The Fair Employment and Housing Act (FEHA) provides for pregnancy disability leave (PDL). There are also the California Family Rights Act (CFRA) and the Kin Care Leave law. The CFRA has the same employee eligibility requirements as the FMLA and applies to the same employers as the FMLA.

Any employer who employs five or more employees must provide PDL to a pregnant employee. PDL provides up to four months of leave and covers prenatal visits, intermittent leave, reduced work schedules, pregnancy, childbirth, or related medical conditions including postpartum depression. An employee is entitled to the same job she had upon returning from PDL. PDL may run concurrently with FMLA leave; however, the leave provided by the CFRA does not begin until PDL has been exhausted. Under the CFRA, an employee is entitled to up to 12 weeks of "baby bonding" time after birth or the placement of a child with the employee for adoption or foster care. The CFRA does not cover pregnancy, and an employee cannot start CFRA leave during pregnancy unless the employee has exhausted her PDL and the employer voluntarily allows the employee to begin her CFRA leave early. If she takes the full PDL and CFRA leave, her total leave will be approximately seven months.

An employer who employs both parents of a child, regardless of their marital status, can limit the total CFRA leave to 12 weeks for both employees in one year. However, if the parents are married then the FMLA does prevent both parents from each taking 12 weeks of FMLA leave upon birth or the placement of the child for adoption or foster care.

An employer is only required to cover medical benefits for the employee during the 12 weeks that are covered FMLA leave, unless the employer covers benefits for other disabilities. California requires that if a company has a Company Disability Leave (CoDL) policy then pregnancy, and the leave associated with it, must be treated the same way other disabilities are treated. An employee using CFRA or FMLA leave is entitled to the same or a comparable job upon return from leave.

In addition to the parental leave provided by CFRA, an employee can use CFRA leave time to care for him/herself, a sick parent, spouse, child or registered domestic partner suffering from a serious health condition. The leave provided by CFRA is the same as that of the FMLA, except the FMLA does not cover domestic partners. Any CFRA leave to care for a sick domestic partner would not exhaust that employee's eligibility for FMLA leave.

California also has Paid Family Leave (PFL) which provides any California employee covered by disability insurance with up to six weeks of benefits if the employee takes leave for baby bonding or to care for the serious health condition of a spouse, domestic partner, child or parent. These payments are similar to short-term disability or unemployment insurance payments.

The Kin Care Leave law applies to any California employers who provide sick leave to their employees. Under the Kin Care law, an employee may use up to half of his/her year's accrued sick leave benefits to care for a sick parent, child, spouse or domestic partner.

California also provides for leave for a parent, grandparent or legal guardian with a child in school. An employee is allowed up to 40 hours per year to participate in school or day care activities of the child. If it is a required school visit then the employee can appear at the visit whenever the school gives advanced notice. In order to be able to take this leave, the employee must provide reasonable advanced notice to the employer, and the employee must use any existing paid time off first.

Colorado

Colorado has a family and medical leave law that applies to State employees only. The Colorado law provides leave for the same reasons as the FMLA. A permanent state employee is eligible for up to 520 hours per year of family and medical leave as long as the employee has been in State service for one year prior to the start of the leave. If an employee is part-time then the employee's amount of family and medical leave will be prorated; for example, a half-time employee is eligible for up to 260 hours of leave per 12-month period. If the employee is a temporary State employee that employee is eligible for prorated leave if he/she has at least one year of service and has worked 1,250 hours in the 12 months prior to the start of the leave. Employees must exhaust their paid leave time and then the rest of their leave will be unpaid.

Connecticut

Connecticut provides eligible employees with up to 16 workweeks of leave during any 24-month period. Covered employers are any who employ 75 or more employees and eligible employees must have worked for the employer for at least 12 months and for 1,000 hours during the 12-month period preceding the leave. An employee may take family and medical leave for the birth of a child, the placement of a child with the employee for adoption or foster care, the employee's serious health condition, or a serious health condition of the employee's spouse, son, daughter, or parent. The employee can elect to, or an employer can require the employee, use accrued paid time off during the leave and, once paid time off is exhausted, the remaining the leave will be unpaid.

For the purposes of the Connecticut family leave law, a parent is biological, adoptive, foster, stepparent, legal guardian of the employee or the employee's spouse, or an individual who stood in loco parentis of the employee when the employee was a son or daughter. A son or daughter is biological, adopted, foster child, stepchild, legal ward, or a person for whom the employee stands in loco parentis and is under the age of 18 or over 18 and incapable of self-care due to mental or physical disability.

Connecticut also provides more family and medical leave to State employees. State employees are entitled to a maximum of 24 weeks of leave in a two-year period. The leave applies in the same instances as the leave provided to other employees in Connecticut, discussed above; however, it also applies if the employee takes medical leave to be a bone marrow or organ donor.

Delaware

Delaware's provisions regarding family leave apply only to State employees. Any State employee who has been employed for one year is entitled to six weeks upon the adoption of a minor child. The employee can also utilize accrued sick leave to travel out of the country for the purposes of adopting a child in a foreign country. Once the adoption is approved the employee's leave would be pursuant to the FMLA. Additionally, State employees are permitted to use sick leave upon the birth of a child or the adoption of a pre-kindergarten aged child.

District of Columbia

The District of Columbia (D.C.) has regulations providing family leave and medical leave for an employee's own serious health condition. Additionally, D.C. has enacted regulations regarding leave for victims of domestic violence and their family members.

D.C.'s family leave law provides 16 workweeks of family leave during any 24-month period. The law applies to all employers, including the District itself, and is available to employees who have worked for the same employer for at least one year without a break in service and for at least 1,000 hours during the 12-month period immediately preceding the leave. The family leave can be used for the birth of a child, the placement of a child with the employee for adoption or foster care, or the placement of a child with the employee for whom the employee permanently assumes and discharges parental responsibility. An employee must use leave to care for a new child within 12-months from the date of birth or placement.

Family leave may also be used to care for an employee's family member with a serious health condition; this leave can be taken intermittently. D.C. defines a family member as a person the employee is related to by blood, legal custody or marriage; a child who lives with the employee and the employee permanently assumes and discharges parental responsibility for; or a person whom within the last year shared a mutual residence with the employee and with whom the employee maintains a committed relationship. The employee and employer can also agree to have the leave taken on a reduced work schedule, not to exceed 24 workweeks.

Family leave may be unpaid, or an employee may use paid time off, but it counts toward the 16 workweeks. If two family members are employees of the same employer, the employer can limit the leave to 16 workweeks total for the same qualifying event. Additionally, the employer can limit the employees to four weeks leave taken simultaneously.

In addition to 16 workweeks of family leave, D.C. employees are also entitled to 16 workweeks within a 24-month period for their own serious health condition. During family or medical leave the employer must maintain an employee's health coverage, but the employee is responsible for continuing to pay the employee's own share of the coverage.

In 2008 D.C. passed the Accrued Sick and Safe Leave Act which provides paid leave time to employees for sick leave or "safe" leave needed as a result of domestic violence, stalking, or sexual assault. The Act applies to all employers, but the number of paid leave days provided depends on the total number of employees. Employers with up to 24 employees must provide three days per year; employers with 25 to 99 employees must provide five days per year; and employers with 100 or more employees must provide seven days per year of paid leave. The paid leave begins to accrue on the employee's first day of work but it cannot be used until the employee has worked for 90 days. The leave can carry over each year, but the employee cannot use more than the yearly maximum in one year unless the employer allows it, and the employee will not be paid for unused time upon resignation or termination.

The paid leave can be used for an absence due to the physical or mental illness of the employee; an absence resulting from obtaining professional medical diagnosis or care; an absence to care for a child, spouse, parent, domestic partner or any other family member of the employee; or an absence resulting from the employee or the employee's family member being the victim of stalking, domestic violence, or sexual assault, provided the absence is directly related to social, legal or medical services pertaining to the event. The Act defines family member as an employee's spouse or person the employee identifies as his/her domestic partner, parents, spouse's parents, children and grandchildren, spouse's children, siblings, spouse's siblings, and a child who lives with the employee and for whom the employee assumes and discharges legal responsibility.

Florida

Florida provides family and parental leave to its State employees. Family leave is leave for a serious family illness or injury, including an accident, disease, or condition, and parental leave is provided to a father or mother to care for a new child who is born or placed with the employee for adoption. The leave is for up to six months, but the State employer cannot require an employee take any family or parental leave.

The State also provides its employees with up to 30 days per year of family leave for non-medical reasons to take care of family responsibilities relating to a child, parent

184

or spouse. Further, State agencies may grant administrative leave of up to one hour per month for employees to participate in family activities such as local school activities (parent teacher conferences), visiting a child in child care centers, or involvement in local school activities like tutoring, guest speaking, career day, or an after school homework center program.

Florida also provides domestic violence leave to all employees who have worked for an eligible employer for at least three months. Eligible employers are those that employ 50 or more employees. An employee is eligible for up to three days leave for activities connected to domestic violence issues. An employee must exhaust other paid time off prior to using this leave unless the employer waives this requirement.

Georgia

Georgia's maternity leave law only applies to employees of the Georgia Public School System. Those employees are entitled to maternity leave of up to one full school year. An employee who chooses to take leave only during the period of physical disability may use her accrued sick leave during this time. An employee who chooses to return to work at the end of the period of disability will need a doctor's certification and will be placed in an equivalent position as per the superintendent. An employee who has been granted leave longer than the period of physical disability is entitled to return to active employment after requesting in writing reassignment as long as there is a vacancy.

Hawaii

Hawaii provides family leave to employees who have worked for six or more consecutive months for a covered employer. A covered employer is one who employs 100 or more employees in Hawaii. For the purposes of Hawaii's family leave law, a child is biological, adopted, foster care, stepchild, or legal ward of the employee (with no age limit). A parent is biological, foster, adoptive, parent-in-law, stepparent, legal guardian, grandparent, or grandparent-in-law. An eligible employee is entitled to four weeks of family leave each calendar year for the birth or adoption of a child or to care for the employee's child, spouse or reciprocal beneficiary, or parent with a serious health condition. Leave to care for a newborn child or newly adopted child must be completed within 12 months from the date of birth or placement. The employer can choose to provide paid leave or allow an employee to use his/her accrued paid time off during the leave. An employee cannot use more than ten sick days, if provided, during the family leave. If both spouses work for the same employer they both get four weeks; it is not capped at four weeks per couple. It is important to note Hawaii's family leave law does not cover an employee's own serious health condition.

Idaho

The following provisions and laws only apply to Idaho State employees. State employees may use their accrued sick time for their own medical purposes or for the serious illness, disability or death of a family member. Covered family members are the employee's spouse, child, foster child, parent, brother, sister, grandparent, grandchild, or any of the same relation by marriage.

186

Idaho provides State employees with Medical, Dental or Optical Appointment Leave (MDA). Employees are allowed up to two hours for each occasional appointment without charge to sick leave for personal or family member medical, dental, or optical exams or treatment. Occasional appointments are those traditionally considered preventative, wellness related or diagnostic. Ongoing treatment for physical or mental illness is not covered by MDA. Public employees are covered by FMLA because the state is considered one employer and employees can take leave under the federal law for ongoing treatment.

Idaho requires all employers treat pregnancy, childbirth and other related medical conditions as temporary disabilities for sick leave purposes.

Illinois

Illinois provides its public employees with four weeks paid maternity or paternity leave to new parents (although a male employee may have to prove paternity if not married to the child's mother) and four weeks paid adoption leave.

Illinois provides unpaid Family Responsibility Leave to public employees. Leave of up to one year is available for the following reasons: 1) nursing or custodial care of an employee's newborn infant, natural or adopted; 2) to care for a temporarily disabled, incapacitated, or bedridden resident of employee's household or family; 3) to furnish special guidance, care or supervision to a resident of the employee's household or a member of the employee's family in extraordinary need thereof; 4)

187

to respond to the temporary dislocation of family due to natural disaster, crime, insurrection, war or other disruptive event; 5) to settle the estate of a deceased member of the employee's family or act as a conservator and the exercise of such functions precludes the employee from working; or 6) to perform family responsibilities consistent with the rest of the Section but not described therein. Family is defined as two or more individuals living under one roof with one head of household, not necessarily blood related, including the employee's spouse; a person of natural relation to the employee such as parent, child, or sibling; or any adoptive, custodial, and in-law individuals when residing in the employee's household. The public employer will continue to pay its share of benefit costs for the first six months if the leave is for reasons 1 through 3 described above, and the employee is responsible for the cost for the rest of the leave or for the entire leave if it is for reasons 4 through 6 described above.

Illinois also provides public employees with child care leave of 1 to 90 days for adoption or other parental reasons including a seriously ill child, an emotionally disturbed child's care, or a similar serious family dilemma. Employees can request an additional 90-day leave which will be deducted from the employee's continuous service.

When an employee returns from Family Responsibility Leave or childcare leave, he/she will be returned to the same or equivalent position.

It is interesting to note that Illinois's Treasury Department extends family medical leave rights to domestic partnerships.

Illinois also provides Family Military Leave to any employee, including independent contractors, who has worked for the same employer for at least 12 months and has worked for 1,250 hours during the 12 months preceding the leave. All employers with at least 15 employees, including the State, are covered. An employee who is the spouse or parent of a person called to service longer than 30 days is entitled to leave. An employer with 15 to 50 employees must provide up to 15 days unpaid leave during the time federal or State deployment orders are in effect. An employer with more than 50 employees must provide up to 30 days' unpaid leave.

Indiana

Indiana's maternity leave applies to Indiana school-teachers. The school may grant a leave of absence for up to one year for pregnancy or childbirth. The teacher's leave may be charged to sick time, at the teacher's discretion, unless a doctor certifies the teacher can perform the regular duties of the job, in that case, the leave is unpaid. The teacher must provide at least 30 days' notice of the intention to take the leave at any time after the commencement of the pregnancy up to one year after the birth of the child. If there is a pregnancy-related emergency then notice is not required to take the leave. The teacher's employment rights remain intact during the leave, and the teacher's group health coverage will continue, although the teacher may have to pay the total premium during any unpaid leave.

Iowa

Iowa law requires employers to treat pregnancy related disability, giving birth, or legal abortion in the same way other temporary disabilities are treated. Additionally, an employer must grant an employee leave for the period of pregnancy-related disability or eight weeks, whichever is less, if the employee provides notice of the need for leave. Employers with at least four employees are covered, but domestic workers and religious institutions are exempt from the law.

Kansas

Kansas law requires employers treat a disability caused or contributed to by pregnancy, miscarriage, abortion, childbirth, and recovery there from as temporary disabilities and in the same way the employer would treat any other employee with a temporary disability under temporary disability insurance or health insurance. Additionally, employers must consider childbearing a justification for a leave of absence for female employees.

Kentucky

Kentucky's family and medical leave law applies only to State employees. It is similar to the FMLA because it has the same requirements that an employee have worked for at least 12 months and 1,250 hours in the 12 months immediately preceding the leave. However, unlike the FMLA, if both parents are State employees they may each take 12 weeks of leave for the birth or placement of a child for adoption or foster care. Kentucky also allows the employee to utilize leave to care for him/herself or an immediate family member with a serious health condition. An immediate family member is the employee's spouse, child, parent, or someone of close blood or legal relationship who resided with the employee for at least 30 days prior to the leave. Lastly, unlike the FMLA which requires FMLA leave to run concurrently with an employee's paid time off, Kentucky State employees can use their accrued paid leave prior to starting the State's provided leave. An employee can choose to keep up to ten sick days instead of exhausting all paid time off before taking family and medical leave.

Kentucky does have an adoption leave law that applies to all employers. It requires an employer to grant an employee reasonable time, not to exceed six weeks, for the reception of an adoptive child under the age of seven. The employee must request the leave in writing.

Lastly, Kentucky provides that teachers in the public school system can be granted a leave of absence not to exceed two consecutive school years for illness, maternity, adoption or disability leave. The teacher resumes his/her contract status prior to leave upon returning from leave.

Louisiana

Employees of parish and city schools in Louisiana are provided 90 days' extended sick leave for each six-year period of employment. The extended sick leave can be used for personal illness or the illness of an immediate family member whenever an employee has no remaining regular sick leave balance. The employee is paid 65% of his/her salary during the extended sick leave. For the purposes of this law a child is biological, adopted, foster, stepchild, or legal ward and a parent is biological or a person who stood in loco parentis for the employee. An immediate family member is the spouse, parent, or child of the employee.

Maine

Maine provides family medical leave to employees who have worked for 12 months for a covered employer. A covered employer is one with 15 or more employees in Maine; the State, including its branches and agencies, and any city, town or municipality, with 25 or more employees. Eligible employees can take family medical leave for a serious health condition of the employee, the birth of the employee's child, the placement of a child 16 or younger with the employee for adoption, to care for a child, domestic partner's child, parent, domestic partner, sibling, or spouse, for organ donation, or for the death or injury of an employee's spouse if the spouse is a member of the military forces. Employees are entitled to up to ten workweeks of leave in any two years unless there are fewer than 15 employees at the worksite. Employees must provide 30 days' notice of their intent to take leave unless it is an emergency.

Maine also provides family military leave to eligible employees. Eligible employees are those who have worked for the same employer for at least 12 months and at least 1,250 hours during the 12 months immediately preceding the leave. All employers with 50 or more employees must provide up to 15 days per year for family military leave only after an employee has exhausted all accrued vacation, personal and compensatory time. Family military leave is that requested by an employee who is the spouse or parent of a Maine resident called to military service longer than 180 days.

Maryland

Maryland requires employers to treat disabilities caused or contributed to by pregnancy or childbirth the same way the employer treats all other temporary disabilities. Additionally, if an employer provides leave with pay to an employee following the employee's child's birth then the employer must provide the same leave to an employee who has a child placed with him/her for adoption.

Maryland also has a leave law that only applies to Maryland State employees. This law allows an employee to use sick leave when a child is placed with the employee for adoption. The employee may use up to 30 days of accrued sick leave immediately following the placement of the child with the employee if the employee is the primary caregiver to the child. An employee who is secondarily responsible for the child may use up to ten days of accrued sick leave immediately following the placement of the child.

Massachusetts

Massachusetts has a Maternity Leave Act whose provisions apply to female employees; however, the Massachusetts Commission Against Discrimination has stated that employers may have to provide the same paternity leave to male employees in order to avoid noncompliance with state or federal discrimination laws. The Maternity Leave Act applies to female employees who have completed their employer's probationary period or, if no probationary period, three months of work. The Act provides employees with up to eight weeks leave for giving birth or adopting a child under the age of 18 or under 23 if mentally or physically disabled. The employee must give the employer at least two weeks' notice of her intention to take leave, and she will be entitled to the same or an equivalent position when she returns. The leave is either paid or unpaid, at the employer's discretion. An employee may be responsible for the cost to continue benefits coverage during the leave.

Employees in Massachusetts are also entitled to 24 hours of leave during any 12-month period in addition to FMLA leave. This additional leave can be used to participate in school activities directly related to the educational advancement of the employee's son or daughter; to accompany a child to routine medical or dental appointments; or to accompany an elderly relative (over the age of 60) to routine medical or dental appointments or other professional appointments related to elder care. An employer can require, or an employee may elect, to substitute accrued personal or vacation time for unpaid leave.

Minnesota

Minnesota employers who grant parental leave to biological parents must also grant time off to an adoptive mother or father. The time off must be at least four weeks leave, or if the employer has a policy for biological parents which provides less than four weeks, that period is the minimum leave adoptive parents must be granted. The period of leave can begin before or at the time of the child's placement, at the discretion of the adoptive parent.

Minnesota also has a parental leave law which covers employers with 21 or more employees at any one site, but for the school leave provisions a covered employer is one who employs one or more persons in Minnesota. Eligible employees are those who have worked at least 12 consecutive months immediately preceding the leave for the average number of hours per week which equals half time for the full time equivalent position in the employee's job classification. For the purposes of this law a child is under 18 years of age or under 20 and still attending secondary school. Eligible employees are entitled to up to six weeks leave to care for a newborn child, either natural or adopted. The leave can being not more than six weeks after the birth or adoption, except in the case where the child must remain in the hospital longer than the mother when the leave cannot begin more than six weeks after the child leaves the hospital. An employee may substitute unpaid leave with paid parental or vacation leave, but not sick leave. If the employee is pregnant she may be entitled to use sick or disability leave if she is sick during the pregnancy or to recover from childbirth. The employee must notify the employer two weeks before his/her return to work if the leave is longer than one month, and the employee will be returned to the same or similar job.

Eligible employees are also entitled to 16 hours unpaid leave a year to attend a child's school conferences, activities, or childcare or other early childhood programs. Employees may use vacation time for this leave.

Further, in Minnesota, employees who work at least halftime are entitled to use accrued sick leave to care for a sick child.

Mississippi

Mississippi provides State employees major medical leave for illness or injury of the employee or an immediate family member. The leave may be used after the employee has used at least one day of accrued personal or compensatory leave for each absence due to illness or one day of leave without pay if the employee has no accrued leave time. Major medical leave may be used for regularly scheduled doctor or hospital visits or for continuing treatment of a chronic disease. The immediate family of an employee includes the employee's spouse, parent, stepparent, child, sibling, stepchild, grandchild, grandparent, son or daughter-in-law, father or mother-in-law, or brother or sister-in-law. An employee's child is any child who is biological, adopted, foster, or for whom the employee stands or stood in loco parentis.

Missouri

Missouri's family leave law applies only to public sector employees. The law allows an employee to use accrued leave or the same leave without pay granted to biological parents to take time off for the purposes of arranging for an adopted child's placement or care for the child after placement. The law also gives stepparents the same rights as biological parents to care for a stepchild. An employee is only eligible for leave if the employee is the person primarily responsible for furnishing care and nurturing the child.

Montana

Montana has a Maternity Leave Act that makes it unlawful for an employer to terminate an employee because of pregnancy or to not grant an employee reasonable leave for pregnancy. The Act also requires employers treat pregnancy-related disabilities the same way the employer treats other disabilities. The Act requires employers return employees to their original jobs or the equivalent of when the employee returns from pregnancy or childbirth leave.

Montana also has an additional leave law that only applies to Montana State employees. It allows an employee to take a reasonable leave of absence and use sick time immediately following the birth or placement of a child for adoption. The leave cannot exceed 15 days if the employee is the birth father or adopting a child, and the leave is up to six weeks for temporary disability resulting from childbirth.

Nebraska

If an employer provides parental leave to its employees for the birth of a child then the employer must provide the same leave to adoptive parents.

Nevada

Nevada has a special law for parents to participate in the academics of their children. The law requires employers grant parents leave to participate in school conferences and other school activities. The parent must be provided four hours per child per school year to attend the activities. The employer can require the employee provide five-days' written notice before leave is to be taken, and the leave does not have to be paid. This law only applies to employers with 50 or more employees in 20 weeks of the current year.

Nevada also requires all employers provide the same disability benefits to an employee with a pregnancy-related disability as the employer provides to all other employees.

Nevada also has a law, for Nevada State employees only, which provides up to 12 weeks of leave to the parent of a child less than six months old or a recently adopted child. The law only applies if the employee is not eligible for FMLA leave.

New Hampshire

New Hampshire has an anti-pregnancy discrimination law that applies to employers who employ six or more employees but does not apply to non-profit religious organizations. An employer must permit a leave of absence to an employee for a period of temporary disability from pregnancy, childbirth, or related medical conditions.

New Jersey

New Jersey has passed its own Family Leave Act (NJ-FLA). Covered employers are those who employ at least 50 employees who have worked for at least 20 weeks during the current or previous year. All employees are counted, whether they are located in New Jersey or not. Eligible employees are those who have worked for the employer for at least one year and at least 1,000 hours, including paid overtime hours, during the 12 months immediately prior to the leave. An employer may deny leave to employees whose base salaries are within the highest five percent of all employees if their absence would have a substantial negative effect on the business. The same is true for the seven most highly paid employees. An employer must provide proper notice to an employee that he/she falls into this category. If the leave has commenced and an employer notifies the employee that he/she meets this exception, the employee must return to work within ten working days.

Eligible employees are provided up to twelve weeks of leave within a 24-month period. The leave is provided to care for a newly born or adopted child, as long as the leave begins within one year of the date the child is born or placed with the employee or to care for the employee's parent, child under 18, spouse or civil union partner who has a serious health condition. Parent means biological, in-law, step, foster, adoptive, or other person who has a parent-child relationship with the employee. Employees may take leave to care for an ill family member intermittently or as a reduced work schedule. Employees may be required to provide 30 days' notice to take leave for the birth or adoption of a child or 15 days' notice to take leave to care for a family member, unless it is an emergency in which case reasonable notice is required. This family leave is separate from any leave an employee may take for his/her own disability. Therefore, if an employee uses federal FMLA leave for his/her own serious health condition, he/she would still have

NJFLA leave available to care for an ill family member or a new child. Another difference between NJFLA and FMLA is that FMLA only applies if the employer employs 50 or more individuals within a 75-mile radius while NJFLA applies if the employer has 50 or more employees nationwide.

New Jersey also provides Family Leave Insurance Benefits. These benefits are temporary disability payments available to employees on leave for their own serious illness or injury or that of an immediate family member. The first seven days of leave are unpaid and then the employee may receive, in a 12-month period, up to 26 weeks of the insurance benefits for one period of the employee's own disability or six weeks for one period of family member temporary disability (42 days if intermittent leave). An employee must have worked 20 base weeks before becoming eligible or earned $7,200. The maximum benefit is $546 per week. These benefits are provided by the State, similar to Unemployment Insurance benefits.

New Jersey State employees are also provided up to 15 days of paid sick leave each year which can be used for the employee's own illness, injury or exposure to a contagious disease, to care for a seriously ill member of the employee's immediate family, or for a death in the employee's immediate family.

New York

In New York, if an employer grants leave for the birth of an employee's child that employer must grant the same leave to an adoptive parent. Additionally, public sector employees may be granted a leave of absence of up to two years for pregnancy and/or childbirth, and that leave of absence can be extended for a period of time not to exceed another two years.

New York employers are prohibited from refusing to employ citizens and residents of the state because they are subject to military duty obligations imposed by federal or state law. Employers may not attempt to have a person waive his or her rights under the law. In certain circumstances, private sector employees who leave a position, other than a temporary position, in order to perform military service, are entitled to reemployment in their previous position or in a position of similar status and pay after the period of military service. This law applies to those employees who receive a certificate of completion of military service, who still are qualified to perform the duties of the position, and who apply for reemployment within 90 days after being relieved of military service. Where the employer's circumstances have so changed during the period of the employee's leave as to make reemployment impossible or unreasonable, employers are not obligated to reemploy these individuals. Private sector employees who take a leave of absence for certain types of military training are required to apply for reemployment within 60 days, or in some situations, ten days, following this training. These rights extended to private sector employees under state law do not apply to persons participating in routine reserve-officer training or corps training, except when performing advanced training duty as a member of a reserve component of the armed forces.

The spouse of a member of the United States Armed Forces, National Guard or Reserves who has been deployed during a period of military conflict, to a com- bat theater or combat zone of operations is entitled to up to ten days of unpaid leave by his/her employer. The leave is available only when the employee's spouse is on leave from the Armed Forces of the United States, National Guard or Reserves while deployed. Coverage of the Spousal Military Leave Law applies to employees employed an average of 20 or more hours per week for employers with 20 or more employees at at least one site.

Employers are prohibited from retaliating against an employee who requests or obtains leave under this law. Employers cannot refuse a leave because of potential adverse effects from the leave, and an employee's vacation days cannot be affected by the employee's decision to take unpaid leave. Further, employees are not required to give advance notice of their intention to take leave under the Spousal Military Leave Law.

With regard to adoption, if an employer allows employees to take a leave of absence upon the birth of a child, an adoptive parent must be entitled to the same leave and upon the same terms.

North Dakota

North Dakota has a leave law for State employees only, which provides the same leave as the FMLA. Additionally, the law states that if an employer provides medical leave to an employee to care for his/her own illness or injury, the employee must be able to use up to 40 hours of sick leave to care for the serious health condition of an immediate family member. For the purposes of North Dakota's law a child is one by birth, adoption, foster care, stepchild, or legal ward less than 18 years old or more than 17 years old and incapable of providing self-care because of a serious health condition.

Ohio

Ohio provides a special leave to an employee if his/her parent, child, or spouse is called to active duty for more than 30 days or is injured, wounded, or hospitalized as a result of military duty. The employee is allowed up to ten days or 80 work hours, whichever is less, for leave to spend time with the family member. The employee must provide 14-days' written notice if the leave is because the person's family member has been called to active duty or two-days' written notice if the leave is due to an injury of the family member. Additionally, the employee can have no other leave time available except for sick or disability leave time in order to take advantage of this leave. This law only applies to employers with 50 or more employees.

Ohio also provides parental leave to Ohio's public employees. State employees can receive six weeks of parental leave time. The employee is paid 70% of his/her salary for the last four weeks of the parental leave. The employee can choose to use paid time off to receive his/her salary during the first two weeks of leave, and to bring his/her pay up to 100% during the other four weeks of the leave.

Oklahoma

Oklahoma has a law regarding family and medical leave for State employees only. The law outlines the FMLA's requirements and guidelines. State employees are free to charge FMLA leave time to accrued annual, sick, compensatory, or donated leave time. Additionally, the state will continue to pay for an employee's health insurance coverage while the employee is on FMLA leave.

Oregon

Oregon provides parental and family leave to eligible employees of covered employers. A covered employer is one who employs 25 or more persons in Oregon for 20 workweeks or more in the current or previous year. Eligible employees are those who have been employed for the 180 days before the leave, and in the case of family leave, they must have worked an average or 25 or more hours per week (this does not apply to parental leave).

Eligible employees are entitled to up to 12 weeks of leave within one year for parental or family leave. Parental leave is leave to care for a newborn or child placed with the employee for adoption or foster care under the age of 18, or over 18 and incapable of self-care because of a mental or physical disability. Parental leave must be taken within 12 months of the birth or placement of the child. Family leave is leave to care for a family member with a serious health condition, leave to care for the employee's own serious health condition, or leave to care for a child with an illness, injury, or condition which is not a serious health condition but requires home care. A family member is the employee's spouse, biological, adoptive or foster parent or child, grandparent or grandchild, parent-in-law, or person with whom the employee was/is in a relationship of loco parentis.

Female employees are also entitled to take 12 weeks of leave for illness, injury, or other condition related to pregnancy or childbirth that disables the employee from performing any job duties. Additionally, an employee who takes 12 weeks of leave in one year to care for a new child (birth, adoption or foster care) may also take 12 weeks to care for a sick child who requires home care. If two related employees work for the same employer, they cannot take concurrent leave unless one is caring for the other or one is caring for a child with a serious illness and the other is suffering from his/her own serious health condition.

Employees are entitled to the same or an equivalent position upon return from leave. An employer can require 30-days' written notice prior to the leave, but in the case of an emergency, the employee only needs to give oral or written notice within 24 hours of commencing leave. An employee may choose to use paid time off to cover some or all of the leave time.

Pennsylvania

Pennsylvania requires that employers treat a disability due to pregnancy the same way they treat other disabilities. Employers cannot mandate that an employee stop work and take maternity leave for a certain period of time. It is the employee's decision when to take maternity leave. Pennsylvania law states an employer may grant leave beyond the disability period for childbearing and requires employers grant childbearing leave equally to male and female employees. Male employees must be able to take the same amount of leave for childbirth that female employees are given.

Rhode Island

Rhode Island provides family and parental leave to eligible employees working for covered employers. A covered employer is one who employs more than 50 employees; the State, and any city, town or municipality employing 30 or more employees. Eligible employees must have worked for 12 months and at least an average of 30 or more hours per week (considered full time). Eligible employees are entitled to up to 13 workweeks of parental or family leave in any two calendar years. Family leave is leave to care for a family member with a serious health condition. Rhode Island defines family members as an employee's parent, spouse, child, parent-in-law, or the employee him/herself, and for employees of the State, it includes domestic partners. Parental leave is leave used for the birth of a child or placement of a child under 16 with the employee for adoption. An employee must provide the employer 30 days' notice of the leave unless prevented from doing so by medical emergency. The employee will be returned to the same or an equivalent position upon return from leave. An employer can require the employee to pay the amount of the health insurance premium for the leave period in advance to the employer, but the employer must return the money within ten days of the employee's return to employment. If an employer allows sick time to be used after the birth of a child, it must also allow sick time to be used for adoption care.

206

Rhode Island also provides family military leave to employees who have worked for at least 12 months and 1,250 hours in the 12 months immediately preceding the leave. The family military leave laws apply to all employers in Rhode Island with at least 15 employees. Family military leave is leave taken by an employee who is the spouse or parent of a person called to military service longer than 30 days. An employer with 15 to 50 employees must provide up to 15 days unpaid family military leave, and an employer with more than 50 employees must provide up to 30 days' unpaid leave. The employee is to provide 14 days' notice if the leave will be five or more consecutive days. The employee will be returned to the same or an equivalent position, and the employee may be responsible for paying for his/her benefits' continuation during the leave.

South Carolina

South Carolina provides additional provisions regarding family medical leave for only State employees. State employees can use up to ten sick days per year to care for ill members of their immediate family. Immediate family means an employee's spouse, children, mother, father, brother, sister, grandparents (and in-laws), grandchildren, and anyone to whom the employee is legal guardian. Additionally, public employees can use up to six weeks of accrued sick leave to care for a child after placement for adoption.

South Dakota

South Dakota provisions state that the adoption of a child by any State employee is to be treated as natural childbirth for leave purposes.

Tennessee

Tennessee provides extended family leave to employees who have worked for their employer for at least 12 consecutive months. The law applies to employers with eight or more employees, the State and any subdivision of the State. Full time employees who meet the 12-month requirement are entitled to take leave for up to four months for adoption, pregnancy, childbirth, or nursing. Adoption leave may begin when the employee receives custody of the child. The employee must give at least three months' advanced notice of his/her intent to take the leave in order to be entitled to be restored to the same or an equivalent position. If the employee's leave must start sooner due to a medical emergency, the employee will not forfeit his/her right to return to the job. The employer determines whether the leave will be with or without pay, but the employee taking the leave cannot have his/her right to other employment benefits altered. The employee can be required to pay for health insurance or other employment benefits, unless it is the employer's practice to pay for these benefits during other types of leave.

In addition to the above law, Tennessee's State employees are entitled to use up to 30 sick days during their four-month leave. State employees can use sick leave for their parental leave or to care for an ill family member.

Texas

Texas laws regarding family and medical leave apply to Texas State employees only. Texas requires employees to use all applicable vacation or sick leave when using FMLA leave, unless the employee is receiving temporary disability or workers' compensation then the employee does not have to use his/her accrued paid time off. If a State employee is not eligible to receive FMLA leave because he/she has not worked the required length of time then that employee is eligible to take parental leave for up to 12 weeks. The employee must use all of his/her accrued paid time off during the leave, and the rest of the leave is unpaid. The leave can begin on the date of the child's birth or the date a child under three years old is placed with the employee for adoption.

Utah

Utah's family and medical leave provisions apply to State employees only. A Utah State employee may use sick leave toward parental leave, adoption care, or the illness or injury of the employee, his/her spouse, children, or parents living with the employee and other FMLA approved purposes. An employee on FMLA leave is responsible for his/her share of benefit payments during the leave. A State employee who is ineligible for FMLA leave, workers' compensation, or long term disability may be granted leave without pay for up to six months cumulative from the first day of the absence. The employee is responsible for the full premium payment for any benefits the employee wants to continue while on the leave.

Vermont

Vermont has a Parental and Family Leave Act which has different requirements for covered employers depending on the leave. A covered employer for parental leave is one with ten or more employees for an average of at least 30 hours per week. A covered employer for family leave is one with 15 or more employees for an average of at least 30 hours per week. An employee is eligible for either parental or family leave if he/she has worked for one year for an average of at least 30 hours per week. An employee is entitled to 12 weeks unpaid leave within a 12-month period for family or parental leave.

An employee may take family leave to care for the serious illness of the employee or the serious illness of the employee's child, stepchild, legal ward who lives with the employee, foster child, parent, spouse, or parent-in-laws. Parental leave may be taken for the birth of the employee's child or the placement of a child under 16 with the employee for adoption. An employee may substitute the unpaid leave with accrued time off, not to exceed six weeks, and it is does not extend the leave provided under the Act. The employee also may still have to pay his/her own contribution to continue health insurance benefits. The employee will be returned to the same or a comparable job when the leave ends.

In addition to the parental and family leave discussed above, Vermont provides short-term family leave to eligible employees. An employee is entitled to unpaid leave up to four hours in a 30-day period and not to exceed 24 hours in a 12-month period. An employer can require this leave be taken in at least two-hour increments. The leave may be taken to participate in pre-school or school activities directly related to academic educational advancement of the employee's child, stepchild, foster child, or legal ward living with the employee; to attend or accompany the employee's child, stepchild, foster child, or legal ward living with the employee to routine medical or dental appointments; to accompany the employee's spouse, parent, or parent-in-law to routine medical or dental appointments; or to respond to a medical emergency involving the employee's child, stepchild, foster child, legal ward living with the employee, parent, spouse or parent-in-law. For this leave an employee must provide seven days' notice to the employer except for medical emergencies. At the employer's discretion, an employee may use paid time off for this leave.

Virginia

Virginia provides State employees with paid family and personal leave. Employees are eligible for 32-40 hours per year of leave depending on their years of service with the State. The family and personal leave is to be used for absences due to short-term incident, illness or the death of a family member, or another personal need.

Washington

Washington has a Family Care Act which allows employees who are provided paid leave to use it to care for a sick family member. For the purposes of the Family Care Act, a family member includes the employee's spouse, registered domestic partner, child, parent, parent-in-law, or grandparent with a serious health condition. An employee may also use paid leave to care for his/her child under the age of 18 with a routine childhood illness or needed preventative care or to care for an adult child with a disability. The Act also allows an employee to use his or her paid leave for the short-term care of a pregnant spouse or domestic partner during or after childbirth. The Family Care Act applies to all employers who provide a paid leave benefit.

Washington has also passed a Family Leave Act which is the same as FMLA except that it includes domestic partners as family members. Additionally, Washington's family leave is in addition to pregnancy disability leave which is determined by the employee's health care provider. For example, if a pregnant employee is deemed to be disabled due to pregnancy or childbirth for six weeks, that employee would still be eligible for an additional 12 weeks of Washington's family leave, even if FMLA leave is exhausted.

Washington has also passed a law providing leave for victims of domestic violence, sexual assault and stalking. An employee can take reasonable leave for legal or law-enforcement assistance, medical treatment, or counseling work, or for safety and relocation related to domestic violence, sexual assault or stalking. Family members (child, spouse, parent, parent-in-law, grandparent, or person the employee is dating) may also take reasonable leave to help a victim. This leave is without pay unless the employer provides paid leave or allows the employee to substitute other accrued paid leave. This leave applies to all employers regardless of their size.

Washington also provides family military leave to any employee who works an average of 20 hours per week for his/her employer. The family military leave law covers all employers. An employee who is the spouse or registered domestic partner of military personnel deployed or on leave from deployment during times of military conflict may take up to 15 days of unpaid leave per deployment.

West Virginia

West Virginia provides family and medical leave to West Virginia State employees and employees of the County Boards of Education. An employee must work for 12 weeks prior to the leave in order to be eligible. Employees are entitled to up to 12 weeks of parental leave, following the exhaustion of all paid time off leave, for birth, adoption, or to care for a child, spouse, parent, or dependent with a serious health condition. During this leave the employee is responsible for paying his/her health insurance premiums.

Wisconsin

Wisconsin provides unpaid family leave to eligible employees working for covered employers. A covered employer is one that employs at least 50 employees, including State offices, departments and agencies. An eligible employee must have worked for the employer for 52 consecutive weeks and 1,000 hours preceding the leave. An employee may take up to six weeks leave in a 12-month period for the birth of a child or the placement with the employee of a child for adoption or as a precondition to adoption. The leave must begin within 16 weeks of the birth or placement. An employee may take two weeks' leave for care for the employee's spouse, child, or parent with a serious health condition. An employee cannot take more than eight weeks in total for any combination of the reasons to take family leave. An employee is also entitled to two weeks medical leave during any 12-month period for his/her own serious health condition.

Wisconsin's law defines a child as biological, adopted, foster, stepchild, or legal ward under the age of 18 or over 18 and incapable of self-care because of a serious health condition. Parent is defined as natural, foster, adoptive, stepparent, or legal guardian of the employee or the employee's spouse. Spouse is defined as the employee's legal husband or wife. When an employee is on leave he/she will have to continue to pay the employee share of his/her health insurance premiums. Once an employee returns from leave he/she will be returned to the same or an equivalent position.

7

Special Rules Applicable to Employees of Schools

Definitions

Certain special rules apply to employees of "local educational agencies," including public school boards and elementary and secondary schools under their jurisdiction, and private elementary and secondary schools. The special rules do not apply to other kinds of educational institutions, such as colleges and universities, trade schools, and preschools. Educational institutions are covered by FMLA, and the Act's 50 employee coverage test does not apply. The usual requirements for employees to be "eligible" do apply, however, including employment at a worksite where at least 50 employees are employed within 75 miles. For example, employees of a rural school would not be eligible for FMLA leave if the school has fewer than 50 employees and there are no other schools under the jurisdiction of the same employer (usually, a school board) within 75 miles.

The special rules affect the taking of intermittent leave or leave on a reduced schedule leave, or leave near the end of an academic term (semester), by instructional employees. "Instructional employees" are those whose principal function is to teach and instruct students in a class, a small group, or an individual setting. This term includes not only teachers, but also athletic coaches, driving instructors, and special education assistants, such as signers for the hearing impaired. It does not include, and the special rules do not apply to, teacher assistants or aides who do not have as their principal job actual teaching or instructing, nor does it include auxiliary personnel such as counselors, psychologists, or curriculum specialists. It also does not include cafeteria workers, maintenance workers, or bus drivers. Special rules which apply to restoration to an equivalent position apply to all employees of local educational agencies.

Limitations on Intermittent Leave

Leave taken for a period that ends with the school year and begins the next semester is leave taken consecutively rather than intermittently. The period during the summer vacation, when the employee would not have been required to report for duty, is not counted against the employee's FMLA leave entitlement. An instructional employee who is on FMLA leave at the end of the school year must be provided with any benefits over

216

the summer vacation that employees would normally receive if they had been working at the end of the school year.

If an eligible instructional employee needs intermittent leave or leave on a reduced schedule leave to care for a family member with a serious health condition, to care for a covered servicemember, or for the employee's own serious health condition, which is foreseeable based on planned medical treatment, and the employee would be on leave for more than 20 percent of the total number of working days over the period the leave would extend, the employer may require the employee to choose either to, a) take leave for a period or periods of a particular duration, not greater than the duration of the planned treatment, or b) transfer temporarily to an available alternative position for which the employee is qualified, which has equivalent pay and benefits and which better accommodates recurring periods of leave than does the employee's regular position. These rules apply only to a leave involving more than 20 percent of the working days during the period over which the leave extends. For example, if an instructional employee who normally works five days each week needs to take two days of FMLA leave per week over a period of several weeks, the special rules would apply. Employees taking leave which constitutes 20 percent or less of the working days during the leave period would not be subject to transfer to an alternative position. "Periods of a particular duration" means a block, or blocks, of time beginning no earlier than the first day for which leave is needed and ending no later than the last day on which leave is needed, and may include one uninterrupted period of leave.

If an instructional employee does not give required notice of foreseeable FMLA leave to be taken intermittently or on a reduced schedule leave, the employer may require the employee to take leave of a particular duration, or to transfer temporarily to an alternative position. Alternatively, the employer may require the employee to delay the taking of leave until the notice provision is met.

Limitations on Leave Near the End of an Academic Term

There are different rules for instructional employees who begin leave more than five weeks before the end of a term, less than five weeks before the end of a term, and less than three weeks before the end of a term. Regular rules apply except in circumstances when:

1. An instructional employee begins leave more than five weeks before the end of a term because of the birth of a son or daughter; the placement of a son or daughter for adoption or foster care; to care for a spouse, son, daughter, or parent with a serious health condition; or to care for a covered servicemember. In this instance, the employer may require the employee to continue taking leave until the end of the term if: a) the leave will last at least three weeks, and, b) the employee would return to work during the three-week period before the end of the term.

2. The employee begins leave during the five-week period before the end of a term because of the birth of a son or daughter; the placement of a son

or daughter for adoption or foster care; to care for a spouse, son, daughter, or parent with a serious health condition; or to care for a covered service-member. In this instance, the employer may require the employee to continue taking leave until the end of the term if: a) the leave will last more than two weeks, and, b) the employee would return to work during the two-week period before the end of the term.

3. The employee begins leave during the three-week period before the end of a term because of the birth of a son or daughter; the placement of a son or daughter for adoption or foster care; to care for a spouse, son, daughter, or parent with a serious health condition; or to care for a covered service-member. In this instance, the employer may require the employee to continue taking leave until the end of the term if the leave will last more than five working days.

Academic term means the school semester, which typically ends near the end of the calendar year and the end of spring each school year. A school may not have more than two academic terms or semesters each year for purposes of FMLA. An example of leave falling within these provisions would be where an employee plans two weeks of leave to care for a family member which will begin three weeks before the end of the term. In that situation, the employer could require the employee to stay out on leave until the end of the term.

Duration of FMLA Leave

If an employee chooses to take leave for periods of a particular duration in the case of intermittent or reduced schedule leave, the entire period of leave taken will count as FMLA leave. In the case of an employee who is required to take leave until the end of an academic term, only the period of leave until the employee is ready and able to return to work may be charged against the employee's FMLA leave entitlement. The employer has the option not to require the employee to stay on leave until the end of the school term. Therefore, any additional leave required by the employer to the end of the school term is not counted as FMLA leave; however, the employer is required to maintain the employee's group health insurance and restore the employee to the same or equivalent job including other benefits at the conclusion of the leave.

Restoration to an Equivalent Position

The determination of how an employee is to be restored to an equivalent position upon return from FMLA leave is made on the basis of "established school board policies and practices, private school policies and practices, and collective bargaining agreements." The established policies and collective bargaining agreements used as a basis for restoration must be in writing, must be made known to the employee prior to the taking of FMLA leave, and must clearly explain the employee's restoration rights upon return from leave. Any established policy which is used as the basis for restoration of an employee to an equivalent position must provide substantially the same protections as required by the FMLA for reinstated employees. In other words, the policy or collective bargaining agreement must provide for restoration to an equivalent position with equivalent employment benefits, pay, and other terms and conditions of employment.

Appendix

Definitions

The following is a summary of the definitional terms provided in the regulations of the FMLA (also available at 29 CFR Part 825) and in other publications of the United States Department of Labor.

Active Duty or Call to Active Duty Status

Duty under a call or order to active duty (or notification of an impending call or order to active duty) in support of a contingency operation pursuant to Section 688 of Title 10 of the United States Code, which authorizes ordering to active duty retired members of the Regular Armed Forces and members of the retired Reserve who retired after completing at least 20 years of active service; Section 12301(a) of Title 10 of the United States Code, which authorizes ordering all reserve component members to active duty in the case of war or national emergency; Section 12302 of Title 10 of the United States

Code, which authorizes ordering any unit or unassigned member of the Ready Reserve to active duty; Section 12304 of Title 10 of the United States Code, which authorizes ordering any unit or unassigned member of the Selected Reserve and certain members of the Individual Ready Reserve to active duty; Section 12305 of Title 10 of the United States Code, which authorizes the suspension of promotion, retirement or separation rules for certain Reserve components; Section 12406 of Title 10 of the United States Code, which authorizes calling the National Guard into federal service in certain circumstances; Chapter 15 of Title 10 of the United States Code, which authorizes calling the National Guard and state military into federal service in the case of insurrections and national emergencies; or any other provision of law during a war or during a national emergency declared by the President or Congress so long as it is in support of a contingency operation.

Administrator

The Administrator of the Wage and Hour Division, Employment Standards Administration, U.S. Department of Labor, and includes any official of the Wage and Hour Division authorized to perform any of the functions of the Administrator.

COBRA

The continuation coverage requirements of Title X of the Consolidated Omnibus Budget Reconciliation Act of 1986, as amended.

Commerce and Industry or Activity Affecting Commerce

Any activity, business, or industry in commerce or in which a labor dispute would hinder or obstruct commerce or the free flow of commerce, and include "commerce" and any "industry affecting commerce" as defined in the Labor Management Relations Act of 1947.

Contingency Operation

A military operation that, a) is designated by the Secretary of Defense as an operation in which members of the armed forces are or may become involved in military actions, operations, or hostilities against an enemy of the United States or against an opposing military force, b) results in the call or order to, or retention on, active duty of members of the uniformed services during a war or during a national emergency declared by the President or Congress.

Continuing Treatment by a Health Care Provider

1. Incapacity and Treatment - A period of incapacity of more than three consecutive, full calendar days, and any subsequent treatment or period of incapacity relating to the same condition, that also involves, a) treatment two or more times, within 30 days of the first day of incapacity, unless extenuating circumstances (circumstances beyond the employee's control that prevent the follow-up visit from occurring as planned by the health care provider) exist, by a health care provider, by a nurse under direct supervision of a health care provider, or by a provider of health care services (such as a physical therapist) under

orders of, or on referral by, a health care provider, or b) treatment by a health care provider on at least one occasion, which results in a regimen of continuing treatment under the supervision of the health care provider. Treatment by a health care provider means an in-person visit to a health care provider, the first of which must take place within seven days of the first day of incapacity. Whether additional treatment visits or a regimen of continuing treatment is necessary within the 30-day period is determined by the health care provider.

2. Pregnancy or Prenatal Care - Any period of incapacity due to pregnancy, or for prenatal care. Absences attributable to this type of incapacity qualify for FMLA leave even though the employee or the covered family member does not receive treatment from a health care provider during the absence, and even if the absence does not last more than three consecutive full calendar days. For example, an employee with asthma may be unable to report for work due to the onset of an asthma attack or because the employee's health care provider has advised the employee to stay home when the pollen count exceeds a certain level. An employee who is pregnant may be unable to report to work because of severe morning sickness.

3. Chronic Conditions - Any period of incapacity or treatment for a chronic serious health condition. A chronic serious health condition is one which a) requires periodic visits (as at least twice a year) for treatment by a health care provider, or by a

nurse under direct supervision of a health care provider, b) continues over an extended period of time (including recurring episodes of a single underlying condition), and, c) may cause episodic rather than a continuing period of incapacity (such as, for example, asthma, diabetes, or epilepsy). Absences attributable to this type of incapacity qualify for FMLA leave even though the employee or the covered family member does not receive treatment from a health care provider during the absence, and even if the absence does not last more than three consecutive full calendar days. For example, an employee with asthma may be unable to report for work due to the onset of an asthma attack or because the employee's health care provider has advised the employee to stay home when the pollen count exceeds a certain level. An employee who is pregnant may be unable to report to work because of severe morning sickness.

4. Permanent or Long-Term Conditions - A period of incapacity which is permanent or long-term due to a condition for which treatment may not be effective. The employee or family member must be under the continuing supervision of, but need not be receiving active treatment by, a health care provider. Examples include Alzheimer's disease, a severe stroke, or the terminal stages of a disease.

5. Conditions Requiring Multiple Treatments - Any period of absence to receive multiple treatments (including any related period of recovery) by a health care provider or by a provider of health

care services under orders of, or on referral by, a health care provider, for a) restorative surgery after an accident or other injury, or b) a condition that would likely result in a period of incapacity of more than three consecutive full calendar days in the absence of medical intervention or treatment, such as cancer (chemotherapy, radiation), severe arthritis (physical therapy), kidney disease (dialysis).

Covered Active Duty in the Armed Forces

For members of a regular component of the Armed Forces this term means duty during deployment of the member with the Armed Forces to a foreign country. Covered active duty for members of the reserve components of the Armed Forces (members of the U.S. National Guard and Reserves) means duty during deployment of the member with the Armed Forces to a foreign country under a call or order to active duty in a contingency operation as defined in Section 101(a)(13)(B) of title 10, United States Code. Prior to the 2010 NDAA amendments, qualifying exigency leave did not apply to employees with family members serving in a regular component of the Armed Forces and there was no requirement that members of the National Guard and Reserves be deployed with the Armed Forces to a foreign country.

Covered Military Member

The employee's spouse, son, daughter, or parent on active duty or call to active duty status.

Covered Servicemember

A current member of the Armed Forces, including a member of the National Guard or Reserves, who is undergoing medical treatment, recuperation, or therapy, is otherwise in outpatient status, or is otherwise on the temporary disability retired list, for a serious injury or illness incurred in the line of duty on active duty. Under the 2010 NDAA amendments, the definition of covered servicemember is expanded to include a veteran who is undergoing medical treatment, recuperation, or therapy for a serious injury or illness if the veteran was a member of the Armed Forces at any time during the period of five years preceding the date on which the veteran undergoes that medical treatment, recuperation, or therapy.

Eligible Employee

An eligible employee is:

1. An employee who has been employed for a total of at least 12 months by the employer on the date on which any FMLA leave is to commence. An employer need not consider any period of previous employment that occurred more than seven years before the date of the most recent hiring of the employee, unless, a) the break in service is occasioned by the fulfillment of the employee's National Guard or Reserve military service obligation (the time served performing the military service must be also counted in determining whether the employee has been employed for at least 12 months by the employer), b) a written agreement, including a collective bargaining

agreement, exists concerning the employer's intention to rehire the employee after the break in service (such as, for example, for purposes of the employee furthering his or her education or for child rearing purposes); and

2. Who, on the date on which any FMLA leave is to commence, has been employed for at least 1,250 hours of service with the employer during the previous 12-month period, except that an employee returning from fulfilling his or her National Guard or Reserve military obligation must be credited with the hours-of-service that would have been performed but for the period of military service in determining whether the employee worked the 1,250 hours of service (accordingly, a person reemployed following military service has the hours that would have been worked for the employer added to any hours actually worked during the previous 12-month period to meet the 1,250-hour requirement). To determine the hours that would have been worked during the period of military service, the employee's pre-service work schedule can generally be used for calculations; and

3. Who is employed in any State of the United States, the District of Columbia or any Territories or possession of the United States.

Eligible employee excludes any Federal officer or employee, any employee of the United States House of Representatives or the United States Senate, any employee who is employed at a worksite at which the employer employs fewer than 50 employees if the total number of employees employed by that employer within 75 miles of that worksite is also fewer than 50, and any employee employed in any country other than the United States or any Territory or possession of the United States.

Employ

To suffer or permit to work.

Employee

This term is defined identically to the term as it is defined in the Fair Labor Standards Act. It refers to any individual employed by an employer. In the case of an individual employed by a public agency it means:

1. Any individual employed by the Government of the United States as a civilian in the military departments in any executive agency (excluding any Federal officer or employee covered under Subchapter V of Chapter 63 of Title 5, United States Code), in any unit of the legislative or judicial branch of the Government which has positions in the competitive service (excluding any employee of the United States House of Representatives or the United States Senate who is covered by the Congressional Accountability Act of 1995), and in a nonappropriated fund instrumentality under the jurisdiction of the Armed Forces, or

2. Any individual employed by the United States Postal Service or the Postal Regulatory Commission; and,

3. Any individual employed by a State, political sub-

division of a State, or an interstate governmental agency, other than an individual who is not subject to the civil service laws of the State, political subdivision, or agency which employs the employee and who a) holds a public elective office of that State, political subdivision, or agency, b) is selected by the holder of such an office to be a member of his personal staff, c) is appointed by such an officeholder to serve on a policy making level, d) is an immediate adviser to such an officeholder with respect to the constitutional or legal powers of the office of such officeholder, or, e) is an employee in the legislative branch or legislative body of that State, political subdivision, or agency and is not employed by the legislative library of such State, political subdivision, or agency.

Employee Employed in an Instructional Capacity

Refer to the definition of Teacher below.

Employer

Any person engaged in commerce or in an industry or activity affecting commerce who employs 50 or more employees for each working day during each of 20 or more calendar workweeks in the current or preceding calendar year, and includes any person who acts, directly or indirectly, in the interest of an employer to any of the employees of such employer, any successor in interest of an employer, and any public agency.

Employment Benefits

All benefits provided or made available to employees by an employer, including group life insurance, health insurance, disability insurance, sick leave, annual leave, educational benefits, and pensions, regardless of whether provided by a practice or written policy of an employer or through an employee benefit plan as defined in the Employee Retirement Income Security Act of 1974. It does not include non-employment related obligations paid by employees through voluntary deductions such as supplemental insurance coverage.

Group Health Plan

Any plan of, or contributed to by, an employer (including a self-insured plan) to provide health care (directly or otherwise) to the employer's employees, former employees, or the families of such employees or former employees. For purposes of the FMLA, the term does not include an insurance program providing health coverage under which employees purchase individual policies from insurers provided that, a) no contributions are made by the employer, b) participation in the program is completely voluntary for employees, c) the sole functions of the employer with respect to the program are, without endorsing the program, to permit the insurer to publicize the program to employees, to collect premiums through payroll deductions and to remit them to the insurer, d) the employer receives no consideration in the form of cash or otherwise in connection with the program, other than reasonable compensation, excluding any profit, for administrative services actually rendered in connection with payroll deduction, and, e) the premium charged with respect to such coverage does not increase in the event the employment relationship terminates.

Health Care Provider

This term refers to, a) a doctor of medicine or osteopathy who is authorized to practice medicine or surgery (as appropriate) by the State in which the doctor practices, or, b) any other person determined by the Secretary to be capable of providing health care services.

Others capable of providing health care services include only, a) podiatrists, dentists, clinical psychologists, optometrists, and chiropractors (limited to treatment consisting of manual manipulation of the spine to correct a subluxation as demonstrated by X-ray to exist) authorized to practice in the State and performing within the scope of their practice as defined under State law, b) nurse practitioners, nurse midwives, clinical social workers and physician assistants who are authorized to practice under State law and who are performing within the scope of their practice as defined under State law, c) Christian Science practitioners listed with the First Church of Christ, Scientist in Boston, Massachusetts (where an employee or family member is receiving treatment from a Christian Science practitioner, an employee may not object to any requirement from an employer that the employee or family member submit to examination (though not treatment) to obtain a second or third certification from a health care provider other than a Christian Science practitioner except as otherwise provided under applicable State or local law or collective bargaining agreement), d) any health care provider from whom an employer or the employer's

group health plan's benefits manager will accept certification of the existence of a serious health condition to
substantiate a claim for benefits, and e) a health care
provider listed above who practices in a country other
than the United States, who is authorized to practice
in accordance with the law of that country, and who is
performing within the scope of his or her practice as
defined under such law.

"Authorized to practice in the State" means that the provider must be authorized to diagnose and treat physical
or mental health conditions.

In Loco Parentis Relationship With Respect to a Child

The definition of son or daughter under the FMLA is
limited to children under the age of 18 or 18 years of
age or older and incapable of self-care because of a mental or physical disability. In loco parentis is commonly
understood to refer to a relationship in which a person
has put himself or herself in the situation of a parent by
assuming and discharging the obligations of a parent to
a child with whom he or she has no legal or biological
connection. It exists when an individual intends to take
on the role of a parent. Under the FMLA, persons who
are in loco parentis include those with day-to-day responsibilities to care for or financially support a child.
Courts have indicated some factors to be considered in
determining in loco parentis status include: the age of
the child, the degree to which the child is dependent
on the person, the amount of financial support, if any,
provided, and the extent to which duties commonly associated with parenthood are exercised.

The fact that a child has a biological parent in the home, or has both a mother and a father, does not prevent an employee from standing in loco parentis to that child. The FMLA does not restrict the number of parents a child may have. The specific facts of each situation will determine whether an employee stands in loco parentis to a child.

Examples of situations in which FMLA leave may be based on an in loco parentis relationship include:

1. A grandfather may take leave to care for a grandchild whom he has assumed ongoing responsibility for raising if the child has a serious health condition.

2. An aunt who assumes responsibility for caring for a child after the death of the child's parents may take leave to care for the child if the child has a serious health condition.

3. A person who will co-parent a same-sex partner's biological child may take leave for the birth of the child and for bonding.

In Loco Parentis Relationship With Respect to a Parent

For FMLA leave purposes, parent is defined broadly as a biological, adoptive, step, or foster parent, or an individual who stood in loco parentis to an employee when the employee was a child. An employee's parents-in-law are not included in the definition of "parent" for purposes of FMLA leave. In loco parentis is commonly understood to refer to a relationship in which a person has put himself or herself in the situation of a parent by assuming and discharging the obligations of a parent to a child with whom he or she has no legal or biological connection. It exists when an individual intends to take on the role of a parent. Under the FMLA, persons who are in loco parentis include those with day-to-day responsibilities to care for or financially support a child. Courts have indicated some factors to be considered in determining in loco parentis status include the age of the child, the degree to which the child is dependent on the person, the amount of financial support, if any, provided, and the extent to which duties commonly associated with parenthood are exercised.

An eligible employee is entitled to take FMLA leave to care for a person who stood in loco parentis to the employee when the employee was a child. The fact that the employee also has a biological, adoptive, step, or foster parent, does not preclude a determination that another individual stood in loco parentis to the employee when the employee was a child. The specific facts of each situation will determine whether an individual stood in loco parentis to the employee within the meaning of the FMLA.

Examples of situations in which FMLA leave to care for a parent may be based on an in loco parentis relationship include:

1. An employee may take leave to care for his aunt with a serious health condition if the aunt was responsible for his day-to-day care when he was a child.

2. An employee may take leave to care for her grand-

mother with a serious health condition if the grandmother assumed responsibility for raising the employee after the death of her parents when the employee was a child.

3. An employee who was raised by same-sex parents, only one of whom has a biological or legal connection with the employee, may take leave to care for the non-adoptive or non-biological parent on the basis of an in loco parentis relationship.

Unless an in loco parentis relationship existed when the employee was a child, an employee is not entitled to take FMLA leave to care for a grandparent, an aunt, or another non-covered relative with a serious health condition.

<u>Incapable of Self-Care</u>

Refers to an individual who requires active assistance or supervision to provide daily self-care in several of the "activities of daily living" (ADL's) or "instrumental activities of daily living" (IADL's). Activities of daily living include adaptive activities such as caring appropriately for one's grooming and hygiene, bathing, dressing and eating. Instrumental activities of daily living include cooking, cleaning, shopping, taking public transportation, paying bills, maintaining a residence, using telephones and directories, using a post office, etc.

<u>Instructional Employee</u>

Refer to the definition of <u>Teacher</u> below.

Intermittent Leave

Leave taken in separate periods of time due to a single illness or injury rather than for one continuous period of time. Intermittent leave may include leave of periods from an hour or more to several weeks. Examples of intermittent leave would include leave taken on an occasional basis for medical appointments or leave taken several days at a time spread over a period of six months, such as for chemotherapy.

Mental Disability

Refer to the definition of <u>Physical or Mental Disability</u> below.

Next of Kin of a Covered Servicemember

This refers to the nearest blood relative other than the covered servicemember's spouse, parent, son, or daughter, in the following order of priority: blood relatives who have been granted legal custody of the covered servicemember by court decree or statutory provisions, brothers and sisters, grandparents, aunts and uncles, and first cousins, unless the covered servicemember has specifically designated in writing another blood relative as his or her nearest blood relative for purposes of military caregiver leave under the FMLA. When no such designation is made, and there are multiple family members with the same level of relationship to the covered servicemember, all such family members are considered the covered servicemember's next of kin and may take FMLA leave to provide care to the covered servicemember, either consecutively or simultaneously. When such a designation has been made, the designated individual shall be deemed to be the covered service-member's only next of kin.

Outpatient Status

As applied to a covered servicemember, this term means the status of a member of the Armed Forces assigned to either a military medical treatment facility as an outpatient or a unit established for the purpose of providing command and control of members of the Armed Forces receiving medical care as outpatients.

Parent

A biological, adoptive, step or foster father or mother, or any other individual who stood in loco parentis to the employee when the employee was a son or daughter. The term does not include parents "in law."

Parent of a Covered Servicemember

A covered servicemember's biological, adoptive, step or foster father or mother, or any other individual who stood in loco parentis to the covered servicemember. The term does not include parents "in law."

Person

An individual, partnership, association, corporation, business trust, legal representative, or any organized group of persons, including a public agency.

Physical or Mental Disability

A physical or mental impairment that substantially limits one or more of the major life activities of an individual. Regulations at 29 CFR part 630, issued by the Equal Employment Opportunity Commission under the Americans with Disabilities Act (ADA), as amended, define these terms.

Public Agency

The government of the United States, the government of a State or political subdivision, any agency of the United States (including the United States Postal Service and Postal Regulatory Commission), a State, or a political subdivision of a State, or any interstate governmental agency. A public agency is considered to be a "person" engaged in commerce or in an industry or activity affecting commerce within the meaning of the FMLA.

Reduced Schedule Leave

A leave schedule that reduces the usual number of hours per workweek or hours per workday of an employee.

Secretary

The Secretary of Labor or authorized representative.

Serious Health Condition

An illness, injury, impairment or physical or mental condition that involves inpatient care or continuing treatment by a health care provider. Conditions for which cosmetic treatments are administered (such as most treatments for acne or plastic surgery) are not "serious health conditions" unless inpatient hospital care is required or unless complications develop. Restorative dental or plastic surgery after an injury, removal of cancerous growths, mental illness or allergies can be considered serious health under certain conditions.

Serious Injury or Illness

An injury or illness incurred by a covered servicemember in the line of duty on active duty that may render the servicemember medically unfit to perform the duties of the member's office, grade, rank, or rating. The 2010 NDAA amended the FMLA's definition of a serious injury or illness as follows: For a current member of the Armed Forces the definition is amended to include not only a serious injury or illness that was incurred by the member in line of duty on active duty, but also a serious injury or illness that existed before the beginning of the member's active duty and was aggravated by service in line of duty on active duty in the Armed Forces that may render the member medically unfit to perform the duties of the member's office, grade, rank, or rating. For a veteran, a serious injury or illness is defined as a qualifying injury or illness that was incurred by the member in line of duty on active duty in the Armed Forces (or existed before the beginning of the member's active duty and was aggravated by service in line of duty on active duty in the Armed Forces) and that manifested itself before or after the member became a veteran.

Son or Daughter

A biological, adopted, or foster child, a stepchild, a legal ward, or a child of a person standing in loco parentis, who is either under age 18, or age 18 or older and "incapable of self-care because of a mental or physical disability" at the time that FMLA leave is to commence.

Son or Daughter of a Covered Servicemember

A covered servicemember's biological, adopted, or foster child, stepchild, legal ward, or a child for whom the covered servicemember stood in loco parentis, and who is of any age.

Son or Daughter on Active Duty or Call to Active Duty Status

The employee's biological, adopted, or foster child, stepchild, legal ward, or a child for whom the employee stood in loco parentis, who is on active duty or call to active duty status, and who is of any age.

Spouse

A husband or wife as defined or recognized under State law for purposes of marriage in the State where the employee resides, including common law marriage in States where it is recognized.

State

Any State of the United States or the District of Columbia or any Territory or possession of the United States.

Teacher, Employee Employed in an Instructional Capacity, Instructional Employee

An employee employed principally in an instructional capacity by an educational agency or school whose principal function is to teach and instruct students in a class, a small group, or an individual setting, and includes athletic coaches, driving instructors, and special education assistants, such as signers for the hearing impaired. This term does not include teacher assistants or aides who do not have as their principal function actual teaching or instructing, nor auxiliary personnel such as counselors, psychologists, curriculum specialists, cafeteria workers, maintenance workers, bus drivers, or other primarily not instructional employees.

Index

Next of Kin of a
Covered Servicemember,
definition of, 63, 239

North Dakota, 202

Notice of Rights and
Responsibilities, 114,
115, 116

Notification(s), 50, 107,
108, 114, 130, 223

Ohio, 203

Oklahoma, 204

On-the-Job Injury, 173

Oregon, 204

Outpatient Status,
definition of, 240

Overtime, 82, 83, 84, 100,
104, 159, 199

Own Serious Health
Condition, 21, 23, 40,
45, 56, 76, 78, 122, 131,
133, 135, 137, 140, 168,
170

Parent, definition of, 62,
240

Parent of a Covered
Servicemember,
definition of, 65, 240

Parent(s), 18, 21, 39, 42,
43, 44, 45, 46, 48, 50,
53, 54, 56, 57, 63, 64,
66, 71, 72, 76, 78, 95,
96, 176, 178, 179, 180,
181, 184, 185, 186, 187,
188, 189, 190, 191, 192,
193, 194, 195, 196, 197,
198, 199, 200, 202, 203,
205, 206, 207, 209, 210,
211, 212, 213, 214, 218,
219, 228, 235, 236, 237,
238, 239

Part-time, 22, 25, 41, 44,
75, 77, 79, 82, 170, 171,
172, 180

Payroll, 25, 27, 31, 88, 91,
92, 158, 159, 233

Pennsylvania, 205

Pension(s), 101, 102, 233

Permanent or Long-
Term Condition(s), and
definition of, 37, 61, 227

Person, definition of, 240

About DataMotion Publishing

We Turn Experts into Authors

D ataMotion Publishing was originally established to provide books, training materials and other published periodicals to Employment Practices Advisors, Inc., a human resources consulting firm.

Now a full service publishing business, DataMotion provides publishing and related support services to subject matter experts ranging from how-to guides, training materials and practitioners resources focusing on the human resources, legal and general business areas.

Services include:
- Manuscript Services
- Interior Book Design Services
- Cover Design
- Marketing and Promotion Services
- Book Website Development and SEO
- Registration Services

257

Our team of experts includes not only publishing and related professionals but also experienced writers and experts in the human resources, legal and business arenas.

www.datamotionpublishing.com
info@datamotionpublishing.com

Also by
Diane Pfadenhauer

*Workplace Investigations: Discrimination
and Harassment*

www.investigateworkplaceharassment.com

The Employer's Guide to New York Employment Laws

www.nyemploymentlawguide.com

*The Employer's Guide to C.O.B.R.A.
Self-Administration*

www.cobralawguide.com

New York State Employer's Legal Guide

www.nyemploymentlawguide.com

* 9 7 8 0 9 8 1 5 8 3 1 7 4 *